" . . . not forsaking . . .
ASSEMBLING TOGETHER . . . "
Hebrews 10:25

Basic Lesson Series—Volume 3

ASSEMBLING TOGETHER

"Exercise thyself unto godliness"
1 Timothy 4:7

WATCHMAN NEE

Christian Fellowship Publishers, Inc.
New York

Available from the Publishers at:

11515 Allecingie Parkway
Richmond, Virginia 23235

PRINTED IN U.S.A.

Basic Lessons—Volume 3

CONTENTS

BASIC LESSONS
ON
PRACTICAL CHRISTIAN LIVING

Burdened with the need of a firm foundation for the Christian life, brother Watchman Nee gave a series of basic lessons on practical Christian living during the training session for workers held in Kuling, Foochow, China in 1948. He expressed the hope that these essential lessons might be faithfully learned by God's people, thereby laying a good foundation for the building up of the Body of Christ.

These messages on practical Christian living have now been translated from the Chinese language and will be published in a series of six books, bearing the various titles of: (1) *A Living Sacrifice*; (2) *The Good Confession*; (3) *Assembling Together*; (4) *Not I, But Christ*; (5) *Do All to the Glory of God*; and (6) *Love One Another*.

"Exercise thyself unto godliness" (1 Tim. 4:7), is the exhortation of the apostle Paul. May our hearts be so exercised by God's Word as to give the Holy Spirit opportunity to perfect the new creation.

All quotations of the Scriptures, unless otherwise indicated, are from the American Standard Version of the Bible (1901).

JOINING THE CHURCH

After one believes in the Lord, he is immediately faced with the problem of joining the church. We mentioned before* how we must be separated from the world. However, that is not the end; there is yet the positive side of joining the church. (We do not like the phrase "joining the church," but use it temporarily to make the issue clear.) It is our desire now to mention four points concerning this matter.

We Must Join the Church

Many believers think they can be Christians all by themselves; they think they have no need to join any church. They say: We want Christ, but we do not want the church. We have our personal relationship with Christ but have no need for a relationship with the church. Can we not pray by ourselves? Surely we can. Can we not read the Bible alone? Doubtless we can. Then why should we go to

* Volume 2, *The Good Confession*, Lesson 9

1

all the trouble of trying to communicate with others? Why not just fellowship alone with the Lord? Because of the need to counteract such thoughts, young believers ought to be shown that they must join the church irrespective of their personal opinions. They should see that there are two sides to salvation.

First, there is the personal side. On the personal side, one may receive life himself and he may also pray to the Lord. He may shut himself in a room and believe in the Lord. But if all that he knows is this personal salvation, he will not develop normally, neither will he persevere, nor will his progress be very great. We have yet to see a hermit-type Christian make much progress. There are those, though, who think that a believer may be like a hermit, hidden in a mountain, disregarding everything except communion with the Lord. We should notice, however, that the spiritual upbuilding of such persons is generally rather superficial; when it comes to a real test or trial, they are unable to stand. When the environment seems favorable, they perhaps keep on, but when the environment turns against them, they are unable to persevere.

There is another side to the Christian life—the corporate side. The Word of God teaches us that from the corporate standpoint, no one can be an independent Christian. As soon as one is saved, he becomes a member of the family of God; he is one of God's children. This is one of the first revelations in the Bible. One who is born again into God's house thus becomes one child amongst many children. The next revelation is that all the saved ones together become God's habitation, the house of God. This house is different from the first house in that it is a dwelling place, whereas the first one is a household. This revelation is further followed by the revelation that all Christians are united as the body of Christ, and they are members one of another. Let us look at these three aspects more closely.

1. WE ARE GOD'S CHILDREN
TOGETHER WITH MANY OTHERS

The life which one receives upon believing in the Lord is a life shared with many other people. If the believer looks even from just one vantage point, whether it be that of the household of God or that of the dwelling place of God or that of the body of Christ, the picture he gets shows that he is but a part of the whole. How then can he desire to live in isolation? To do so surely means to miss the fulness in God. He may seek to maintain fellowship with God, yet he will miss out on much if he is not properly joined together with others. He will not be able to fully emit the light of the highest and most abundant life, for it is only in the church that fulness is found.

How can one be in a family of five brothers and sisters and have no communication with them? If I am the only child in the family, I cannot maintain any contact with my other brothers and sisters for I have none. But if I am not an only child, but one among five, just a part of the family, how dare I suggest that I will not have any relationship with my brothers and sisters but will be my father's only child? Can I shut myself in a room and tell the rest of the family not to bother me because I am my father's only child? Can I then have nothing to do with the rest of them?

When one believes in the Lord, he does not become an only begotten son; he is rather one son among tens of thou-

3

sands. This very fact eliminates the possibility of shutting oneself up solely to the Father. Though you may be born as an only child in an earthly family, yet when you believe in the Lord, you are born again into the biggest family in the world. No family can be bigger than this family of God, for it includes countless numbers of brothers and sisters. Do not despise them because there is such a great multitude of them; seek rather to know them and to communicate with them since you yourself are one of them. If you have no desire at all to see your brothers and sisters, I wonder if you are really a brother or sister in the Lord. How can one who is born of God not be moved in his heart by those who are also born of God? Can he refuse to give them the right hand of fellowship?

It is not a Christian concept for a person to be only concerned with his own welfare. Being in the family, one has to be a brother to the brothers, a sister to the sisters. Such a relationship comes from the life of God and is filled with love. Who does not long for his brothers and sisters, who does not desire to see them and have fellowship with them? This is a wonderful thing!

Please remember: though you receive the life of God personally, yet the life you receive belongs to tens of thousands of the children of God; yours is but a part of the whole. The very nature of your new life is not independence—it requires you to fellowship with the rest of the brethren.

2. THE CHURCH IS GOD'S HABITATION

Let us now turn to the second point. The Bible reveals to us a most wonderful thing when it shows us that the church is the habitation of God. This is found in Ephesians 2.

4

All the revelations in Ephesians are of tremendous dimensions and this one in chapter 2 is one of them. We must know that God has a dwelling place, a habitation on earth. The thought in the Bible of a habitation for God starts with the tabernacle and continues right on up to the present. In the past God dwelt in a magnificent house, the temple of Solomon. Now He dwells in the church, for today the church is God's habitation. We, the many, are joined together to be God's habitation. As individuals, though, we are not so. It takes many of God's children to be the house of God in the Spirit. This agrees with what 1 Peter 2:5 says, "Ye also, as living stones, are built up a spiritual house. . . ."

How is this spiritual house built? It is with living stones, not dead ones. Solomon's temple was built with dead stones, but today God's house is made with living stones. Peter was a living stone, for this is the meaning of his name. By putting these living stones together, God gets His temple. Can one believer alone be a house? If there are no stones built on other stones, it is not a good sign, for it expresses the idea of ruin. It speaks of the desolation that comes after judgment when no stone is left standing on another stone. If a house is to be constructed, stones must be built on stones and stones must be joined to stones. Thank God, you are saved, you have trusted in the Lord Jesus, you are now a stone. Don't then just hide your stone away some place by itself. Let your stone be built together with the other stones and you will have a house. For the stones to be left scattered and independent is not only useless but also can become a cause of stumbling.

As soon as one believes in the Lord, he becomes one of the stones in God's habitation. He is a stone, but until he is

5

related to other stones, he is useless. It is like the parts of an automobile. The car can run only when the many parts are put together. What use does one have if he remains alone? He will lose out on the riches of God. We dare not say that living stones standing alone become dead stones, but it is certainly true that a stone, though living, will lose its usefulness and miss out on spiritual riches if it is not joined to other stones to become God's habitation. We can contain God's richness only when we are joined together with other living stones; then God can dwell in our midst. That is why there should be a conviction in our hearts that we must be in the church.

It is marvelous to know that one is saved. I remember I once read what Mr. Stoney said approximately one century ago, "A most wonderful thing happened after I was saved. One day I knew I was a piece of material for the building of the dwelling place of Christ. It was most wonderful to me." When I read it that day, I felt this statement was rather common; I could not see the wonder of it. But as I recall it today, I concur with him wholeheartedly. If one really sees what Mr. Stoney saw, he will most surely be touched by the marvel of it.

Thank God, we are truly material for Christ's spiritual house. If any of these materials are severed from the house, they will turn totally useless. To see this is something simply grand. Think how indispensable is this little piece of stone that I am to God's dwelling place, the want of which will create a hole in the house for the thief to climb in! I am God's material; He cannot do without me!

Therefore, beloved, you must see that you have been brought in by the Holy Spirit to be material for the building of God's temple. How useless you are if you shut yourself away from others. The purpose of a piece of material is to be joined with other material. For the material to be alone deprives it of its function. To be independent is to miss out on the riches God intended you to enjoy, for you will not be able to contain God. To contain God, we need to be joined together. For example, suppose we have many wooden barrels here. They were made by putting pieces of wood together. We may use these vessels for carrying water. But if we take out a piece of wood, can we carry water with that one piece? Certainly not. The quality of the wood has not changed, but its fulness is lost. It can be dipped into water, yet it cannot transport water. Its richness has been lost. Likewise, we are God's house; we cannot afford to be independent lest we lose out on the riches of God.

As young believers, you may not grasp this fully; yet as time goes on, you will. In fact, the moment you believe in the Lord, you do have within you a natural inclination to meet with God's children. Spontaneously you seek to find other stones. You should simply follow this inward urge and not let the thoughts of your mind prevent you from joining with other believers.

3. TOGETHER WE BECOME THE BODY OF CHRIST

We are one in the body of Christ; we have become one body—the body of Christ. "There is one body . . ." (Eph. 4:4). "For as the body is one, and hath many members, and all the members of the body, being many, are one body; so also is Christ" (1 Cor. 12:12). These words show us how absolutely impossible it is for one to be independent.

As a member of a human family, I can refuse to have

7

anything to do with my brothers and sisters if I am so peculiar that I want to cultivate a relationship with my father as if I were an only child. Likewise, though I am a living stone among many stones to be made into God's habitation, I can also be so eccentric as to be unwilling to be built up together with others. Peter was a living stone even before he was built up with others, but he was just a single stone. Perhaps it is my desire to be a Christian all by myself and to not care whether there is a hole in the house. Yet God further shows us that we are more than stones in the house or brothers and sisters in the family; we are one body. You may be an eye, a mouth, a hand, a foot, or whatever, in the body. An eye is very useful to the body, but if it is left at home, it is useless. A hand joined to the arm is effective, but it will be ineffective if put in a glass container. A foot fitly framed in the body is of great service, but what will it be worth if it is left upstairs? The body is such that no member may be severed from it and remain useful. The relationship of each part to the other is most direct and intimate.

If you were to visit a house and see a leg on the table, a hand under the chair, and an ear on the floor, you would never visit that house again. How repugnant it would be to pick up a hand, a mouth, a nose, an eye, or an ear from off the road. Whatever is of the body cannot be separated. God's family may be forcibly broken up, God's temple may also be destroyed, but the body of Christ cannot be separated. Neither the ear nor the hand nor the foot can angrily declare its independence. No, all the members of the body must be joined together in one.

The Lord has not given to any one person the whole fulness of life. The life we receive does not allow us to be independent, for our life is dependent on the life of others. It is a dependent life: I depend on you and you depend on me. Do remember that no member can afford to be independent, for independence means certain death. Isolation takes away life as well as fulness.

Therefore we expect young believers to realize that they must be joined to other Christians. They should not be Christians for several years and still remain alone.

God has not given us an independent life. We are mutually attached. You have heard of subsidiary institutions or subordinate persons. All Christians are like that—subordinates, for no one is able to stand isolated before God. All of us subsist on the lives of other Christians. We have seen this only after many years of learning. Our hope for young believers is that they may begin their life as subordinates. Thus they shall be plentifully supplied with love and fellowship.

A Christian therefore must join the church. Now this term, "joining the church," is not a scriptural one. It is borrowed from the world. What we really mean is that no one can be a private Christian. He must be joined to all the children of God. For this reason, he needs to join the church. He cannot claim to be a believer all by himself. He is a Christian only by being subordinate to the others.

Which Church I Should Join

It is necessary to join the church, but which church should I join? Because of the many different churches existing today, this matter creates a very real problem.

Over the two thousand years of church history, various churches have been raised up at different times. This we may call the cause of time. Then as churches have been formed in different areas, area has become a cause. Also, with the raising up of different human instruments used in the planting of churches, people have become a cause. In addition to these three causes of time, area, and person, there is further the cause of emphasis on a particular truth in the Bible. The Word of God contains so many aspects of truth that people tend to establish churches based on one special truth. Maybe in a certain area there arises a special need and someone comes forth with a particular emphasis on one aspect of truth; consequently a different church is organized. The result is that that particular emphasis may become another cause of dissent.

Based on the various conditions mentioned above, many churches have been produced. The number of churches in the world today exceeds fifteen hundred. These are all well-organized and approved. They are not reckoned according to locality but according to a system. Brethren, when we advise believers to join the church, we are faced with the formidable task of choosing one from among fifteen hundred churches.

Let us consider this matter before God. Is there a way out of the confusion? We believe there is, for the Word of God still remains with us. We can search the Scriptures and find out what God has to say about this. Indeed, God's Word *has* already revealed His appointed way as to which church we ought to join. There is no need for us to spend much time investigating and inquiring into the many different churches. If we had to analyze and research all of them, we would probably never in our lifetime be able to solve the problem because we have neither the strength nor facility to do it. Yet God has not left us in the dark. The Bible clearly indicates to us the way we should follow.

God's Way Is the Local Church

The Bible gives the simplest guideline concerning the church. It is clear and unconfused. If we read the beginning verses of the epistles, the Acts, and the first chapter of Revelation, we meet such names as "the church which was in Jerusalem" (Acts 8:1), "the church of God which is at Corinth" (1 Cor. 1:2; 2 Cor. 1:1), and "the seven churches that are in Asia" (Rev. 1:4), which are the church in Ephesus, the church in Smyrna, the church in Pergamum, the church in Thyatira, the church in Sardis, the church in Philadelphia, and the church in Laodicea (Rev. 2:1, 8, 12, 18; 3:1, 7, 14). In the Bible the churches are divided, but what makes the division? One and only one rule divides the church. Anyone can see the answer, for it is crystal clear.

The Bible permits the church to be divided solely on the ground of locality. Corinth is a city, so are Ephesus, Colosse, Rome and Philippi. All the churches are divided wholly according to locality. In a word, churches can only be divided according to locality, not by any other factor. A locality, a city, is the unit. As Corinth, Ephesus, and Colosse are all cities, so the boundary of the church is the city. Locality constitutes the basic unit.

The smallest church takes a locality as its unit; so does the biggest church. Anything smaller than a locality may not be considered a church, nor can it be so recognized if it is bigger than a locality. This is very clear in 1 Corinthians 1.

There it mentions the church which is in Corinth. When some people in the church at Corinth specify themselves as of Cephas, of Paul, of Apollos, and of Christ, they divide the church into four parts. This makes the church too small, so Paul chides them for their divisions. Paul is good, Apollos is good, Cephas is good, but it is not good to divide according to these men. The church may be divided only according to locality, not according to the apostles. Division according to the apostles is condemned by the Bible as being divisions in the flesh. Such division results in sects.

However, neither should the scope of the church exceed that of a locality. In reading the Bible, we find "the churches of Galatia" (Gal. 1:2), "the churches of Asia" (1 Cor. 16:19; see also Rev. 1:4), and "the churches . . . throughout all Judea" (Acts 9:31 Authorized Version). There were many churches in Judea, in Galatia, and in Asia; hence in Acts they were called the churches in Judea, in Galatians the churches in Galatia, and in Revelation the churches in Asia. Judea was originally a nation, but at that time it had become a Roman province. The various churches in the different localities of that province could not be combined to form one church, so the record in Acts terms them the churches throughout Judea. Galatia was also a Roman province, not just a city. There were a number of churches in that place too; consequently the plural of the word "church" was used to designate the churches in Galatia. These churches were not named "The Church in Galatia," thus showing that the church should not be bigger in boundary than a locality. In the same vein, the churches in Asia were mentioned not in the singular but in the plural form. Ephesus, Smyrna, Pergamum, Thyatira, Sardis, Philadelphia, and Laodicea were seven localities in Asia. They were not united together as one big church; rather they remained seven churches.

It is quite clear from the Bible that a church may be designated only by the name of the locality in which it is located. It should not be named according to a man or doctrine or system or history. No distinction is allowed on the basis of men, of nations, or of doctrines. The Word of God permits only the distinction of locality. Wherever one sojourns, he belongs to the church in that locality. To change his church affiliation, he has to move somewhere else. God recognizes the distinction of locality alone; He will not justify any other basis.

How We Join the Church

Finally, let us ask the question—how do we join the church? Never once in the Bible do we find the phrase "join the church." It cannot be found in Acts nor is it seen in the epistles. Why? Because no one can join the church. To join means that one is still outside. Can an ear decide to join my body? No, if it is in my body, it is already joined. If it is not already in my body, then there is no way for it to join. We do not join the church. Rather, we are already in the church and therefore are joined to one another.

When, by the mercy of God, a man is convicted of his sin and through the precious blood is redeemed and forgiven and receives new life, he is not only regenerated through resurrection life but is also put into the church by the power of God. It is God who has put him in; thus he already is in the church. He *is* an insider, so he has no need of joining. Many think of joining the church. Let it be known, however, that whatever can be joined is not the real thing. One cannot join the true church of God even if he would like to. If he is of the Lord, born of the Holy Spirit, then he is already in the church and has no need to join it.

Therefore it is neither necessary nor possible to join the church. No one can enter into the church by joining it; those who are already in do not need to join. The very desire to join reveals the fact that one is still on the outside. The church is so special that it cannot be joined. The determining factor is whether one is born of God. If one is born of God, he is already in; if he is not born of God, there is no way to join. Is not this corporate body wonderful? It cannot be joined by signing a decision card or by taking a test. All who are born of God are already in the church; therefore they have no need to join it.

Then why do we persuade you to join the church? We are only borrowing this term for the sake of convenience. You who have believed in the Lord are already in the church, but your brothers and sisters in the church may not know you. You have believed, but the brethren may not know it. You are redeemed, yet the church may not be aware of it. Since belief is something in the heart, it may not be known to others. For this reason we must seek fellowship, just as Paul sought to receive the right hand of fellowship from those in the church at Jerusalem (Gal. 2:9). We must go to the church, telling them that we too are Christians and asking them therefore to receive us as such. Since men are limited in knowledge, they need to be told that we are brothers and sisters in order that they may receive us. This is not, however, the same thing as the popular sense of joining the church.

Since my father is a Chinese, I do not need to be naturalized to be a Chinese. But upon becoming a believer, yet unknown to the church, I should go to the church and ask to be recognized and to be given fellowship. If the brethren find out that I am indeed one of them, that I am a true believer, they then will give me the fellowship I seek. This is the true sense of joining the church.

You who are already in Christ should learn to seek the fellowship of the children of God. With this fellowship of the body you may serve God well. If you as young believers can see this light, you will move a step forward in your spiritual path. Thank God for His mercy.

LAYING ON OF HANDS

Wherefore leaving the doctrine of the first principles of Christ, let us press on unto perfection; not laying again a foundation of repentance from dead works, and of faith toward God, of the teaching of baptisms, and of laying on of hands, and of resurrection of the dead, and of eternal judgment.

Heb. 6:1–2

Now when the apostles that were at Jerusalem heard that Samaria had received the word of God, they sent unto them Peter and John: who, when they were come down, prayed for them, that they might receive the Holy Spirit: for as yet it was fallen upon none of them: only they had been baptized into the name of the Lord Jesus. Then laid they their hands on them, and they received the Holy Spirit.

Acts 8:14–17

And when they heard this, they were baptized into the name of the Lord Jesus. And when Paul had laid his hands upon them, the Holy Spirit came on them; and they spake with tongues, and prophesied.

Acts 19:5–6

17

Behold, how good and how pleasant it is
For brethren to dwell together in unity!
It is like the precious oil upon the head,
That ran down upon the beard,
Even Aaron's beard;
That came down upon the skirt of his garments;
Like the dew of Hermon,
That cometh down upon the mountains of Zion:
For there Jehovah commanded the blessing,
Even life for evermore.

Ps. 133

And he shall lay his hand upon the head of the burnt-offering; and it shall be accepted for him to make atonement for him. . . . And he shall lay his hand upon the head of his oblation, and kill it at the door of the tent of meeting: and Aaron's sons the priests shall sprinkle the blood upon the altar round about. . . . and he shall lay his hand upon the head of his oblation, and kill it before the tent of meeting: and Aaron's sons shall sprinkle the blood thereof upon the altar round about. . . . and he shall lay his hand upon the head of it, and kill it before the tent of meeting; and the sons of Aaron shall sprinkle the blood thereof upon the altar round about. . . . And he shall bring the bullock unto the door of the tent of meeting before Jehovah; and he shall lay his hand upon the head of the bullock, and kill the bullock before Jehovah. . . . And the elders of the congregation shall lay their hands upon the head of the bullock before Jehovah; and the bullock shall be killed before Jehovah. . . . And he shall lay his hand upon the head of the goat, and kill it in the place where they kill the burnt-offering before Jehovah: it is a sin-offering. . . . And he shall lay his hand upon the head of the sin-offering, and kill the sin-offering in the place of burnt-offering. . . . And he shall lay his hand upon the head of the sin-offering, and kill it for a sin-offering in the place where they kill the burnt-offering.

Lev. 1:4; 3:2, 8, 13; 4:4, 15, 24, 29, 33

Biblical Teaching and Example

The Bible clearly shows us the need for baptism. It also very clearly indicates the need for the laying on of hands. In both Samaria and Ephesus, the believers had the laying on of hands after baptism. This was what the apostles did in their time. Likewise, in our time the children of God will incur loss if they are only baptized but do not have the laying on of hands.

"Wherefore leaving the doctrine of the first principles of Christ, let us press on unto perfection" (Heb. 6:1), exhorts the writer of Hebrews. In Christian life, there are a few truths which are foundational. A foundation needs to be laid only once, but it must be firmly laid. What is it that is included in the doctrine of the first principles of Christ? Not only are repentance, faith, resurrection, and judgment listed, but also baptism and the laying on of hands. These two, then, are also foundational truths in Christianity. Our foundation will not be complete if the laying on of hands is missing.

The error of the church today is quite different from that of the Hebrews in the first century. The Hebrews, having laid the foundation, circled around and never went beyond it. Today, though, we go forward without ever having laid the good foundation.

Because those to whom the apostle wrote revolved all the time around such things as repentance and faith, baptism and the laying on of hands, resurrection and judgment, he exhorted them to leave the doctrine of the first principles of Christ and press on to perfection. But today's Christians move too fast; we run away before the foundation has been laid. The apostles had to persuade people to leave, whereas we must induce people to return.

The Meaning of the Laying on of Hands

We have already seen what baptism has done for us. It calls us out of the world and thus delivers us from the world. It identifies us with Christ so that we may share in His resurrection. What, then, can the laying on of hands do for us? What is its meaning?

In the old Testament we find that the laying on of hands has a double significance. It is mentioned most frequently in Leviticus, chapters 1, 3, and 4, so we will look there to find its first meaning.

1. IDENTIFICATION

The laying on of my hand on the head of the sacrifice in Leviticus 1 signifies that I am identified with the sacrifice and the sacrifice with me. Why do I not offer myself to God, but offer a bullock instead? "For every beast of the forest is mine, and the cattle upon a thousand hills" (Ps. 50:10), says the Lord. What is the use of bringing cattle or sheep to Him? God does not lack a bullock or a lamb. It is men that He wants to offer themselves.

But what would happen if I actually came to the altar and offered myself? I would be doing the same thing as the Gentiles did, as those who worshiped Moloch. In the Old Testament, there were people who served Moloch. Instead of offering cattle and sheep, they sacrificed their own sons and daughters on the altar to their god. Does our God desire only cattle or sheep? If we offer ourselves to God, how is our God different from Moloch? He is different in that Moloch demanded the blood of our sons and daughters, but our God requires us to offer ourselves. His charge is even more severe than that of Moloch.

It is true that God's demand is more strict, but He shows us a way whereby we may sacrifice and yet not be burned. How? I bring a bullock or a lamb to the Lord. I lay my hand upon the head of the sacrifice. Whether I pray audibly or silently, my prayer is: This is I. I myself should be on the altar and be consumed by fire. I myself ought to be sacrificed, and I would indeed gladly offer myself to You. I should offer myself to be a burnt-offering, a sweet savor unto You. Lord, I now bring this bullock with me, and upon its head I lay my hand. By doing this, Lord, it signifies that this bullock is I, and I am this bullock. When I ask the priest to slay it, it is as if I am slain. When the blood of the bullock flows, my blood flows. When the priest sets the sacrifice on the altar, he has put me on the altar. I have laid my hand on it, so it is I.

Is not the same principle of identification illustrated in baptism? When I step into the water, I say this is my grave, for the Lord has buried me in it. I take the water as my grave. Likewise, as I lay my hand on the head of the bullock, I take the bullock as myself. When I offer it to God, I offer myself. The bullock stands for me.

Hence, the first meaning of the laying on of hands is identification. This is its prime significance in the Old Testament. I am identified with the sacrifice and it is I. Today both the sacrifice and I stand in the same position. When it is brought to God, I am brought to God.

2. IMPARTATION

There is a second significance to the laying on of hands in the Old Testament. In Genesis we see how Isaac laid his hands on his two sons*, and how Jacob laid hands on his two grandsons, Ephraim and Manasseh (48:8-20). Jacob laid one hand on each of his grandsons and blessed them. So the laying on of hands becomes the impartation of blessing. With whatever blessing one is blessed, it shall come to pass.

In short, the significance of the laying on of hands is twofold: identification and impartation. These two may again be summed up by another word, communion. Through communion, we become identified; through communion, what one person has flows to another person.

Why Christians Must Have the Laying on of Hands

We now proceed to ask: Why should Christians have the laying on of hands? Why does the Bible show us this act performed by those who are representative of the body? Why do the apostles lay hands on believers after the latter are baptized?

To answer these questions, we need to explain first what is meant by the body of Christ and what the anointing oil refers to. Let us read 1 Corinthians 12:12–13 together with Psalm 133. Christianity is really a marvel. The marvel lies in God's intention to secure on earth a man who is absolutely obedient to Him, who can fully represent Him and who lives out His life exclusively. Today God has already

---

* Editor's note: Implied in chapter 27:27–40.

set up this man to be Christ and Lord. "Let all the house of Israel therefore know assuredly, that God hath made him both Lord and Christ, this Jesus whom ye crucified" (Acts 2:36). God poured out His own Spirit upon this Man, Jesus of Nazareth, as the Head. In other words, the Lord Jesus does not receive the anointing oil as an individual but as the Head of a corporate body. As the Holy Spirit is poured upon Him, the Head, the same Spirit is poured on the body which is the church. Thus He receives God's anointing for the sake of the body.

His name is Christ (*Christos*—the Anointed One), and our name is Christian (*Christianos*—belonging to the Anointed One). He is the Head, and the church is the body. God does not intend to create only one individual; His desire is for a corporate man. If the church were left to herself, she could not possibly satisfy God's heart nor could she maintain God's testimony, for she herself has no strength. That is why God must pour His oil upon the church. With the oil, she can satisfy God's demand, for the oil represents God's authority. The authority of God is given to the church through the anointing oil.

Let it be noticed, however, that God's oil is not poured on any one member nor does it fall on all the members; rather it is sent to the Head. The Holy Spirit is given to the Head, not to the body. But as the Head receives the oil, the whole body is anointed. Do we see the difference here? The concern is not how each individual member receives the Holy Spirit, nor how all the members receive the Holy Spirit, but how the Head is anointed.

How, then, are we to receive the oil? If we stand in the body, the oil which has been poured on the Head will naturally come to us. Since the oil is not given to individuals,

23

it is impossible for us to receive the anointing on an individual basis. This does not mean that we will not be individually anointed; it simply asserts that we cannot ask for individual anointing. The difference involved here is great. Many fail to receive blessings from God because they seek the Holy Spirit on an individual basis.

When the precious oil was poured upon Aaron's head, it ran down upon his beard and down to the skirt of his garments. Aaron's skirt was quite long, for it covered his feet. In other words, the oil which is poured on the head flows to the lowest part of the body. It is, therefore, clear that people enjoy the anointing oil today not because of their personal condition before God but because of their standing in the body. If we stand in our place beneath the Head, the oil will most assuredly come down upon us. Receiving the oil is not merely a personal matter nor even a body affair, but strictly a matter of taking a position in the body under the Head.

It is imperative as we travel the spiritual road, that we have the power of the Holy Spirit in order to testify. Otherwise we will witness in the flesh. The holy oil is never poured on human flesh. This is a point we need to take note of. We cannot do anything according to our own thought; we must have the anointing oil. Whether we have it depends on our having a proper relationship with the body. It does not rely upon our asking or our prayer.

Let it be re-emphasized: the Bible never teaches that the body is anointed. It only mentions that the Head is anointed. The body is anointed because the Head is anointed. If the body wants to be anointed independently, it will never receive the anointing. The precious oil is poured on Aaron's head, not on his body, though it does then flow down over the whole body from the beard to the skirt. Only the ignorant will seek individual anointing; only the simple will look for an independent anointing. Whoever is subject to the Head by standing in his particular place in the body as appointed by the Head will receive the anointing oil.

The Apostles Laid Hands on Believers

The Word of God shows us how after one is baptized into Christ, he receives the laying on of hands through those who are God's appointed authority, such as the apostles. The apostles represent the Head, Christ, as well as the body of Christ. When one receives the laying on of hands, he bows his head and worships, for hereafter he will never again raise his own head but will submit himself under authority. His own head is no longer head; instead he is under authority.

The apostles represent the body. As they lay hands on the believers, it is as if they are saying that we all have fellowship with one another for we are one. "And God hath set some in the church, first apostles" (1 Cor. 12:28a). Being first, they can very well represent the church. By the laying on of their hands, they declare to the believers: "Brethren, you are one with the body of Christ, therefore the precious oil which flows down from the Head comes to you."

The apostles also represent Christ. "First apostles"—the "first" here implies authority; that is to say, they are delegated authorities of the Head. So when they lay hands on the believers, it is equivalent to the laying on of the Lord's hands. Through their hands, not only the church but also

25

Christ has laid hands on the Christians. Henceforth, we are subject to the authority of Christ the Head.*

How to Receive the Laying on of Hands

We find that the meaning of the laying on of hands has two aspects: identification and impartation. The laying on of hands in the first aspect joins a person to the body and in the second aspect communicates what the Head has for the member. It requires being a member in the body as well as being subject to the authority of the Head. No one can say he is sufficient alone. The new life which he receives is corporate in nature; it does not allow independence. In the body, he lives; out of the body, he dies. On the basis of this identification is the impartation of blessing.

If a brother lays hands on me, it is not a meaningless or indiscreet act. My eyes must be opened to see that hereafter I am but a child among many children, a cell among many cells, one member among many members. I live by the life of the body just as in this physical body every member lives by the whole body. If I act independently, I come to an end and thus will be useless. If I cease to fellowship with other children of God, something is drastically wrong with me. No matter how strong I am, I cannot exist all by myself. If I am cut off from the body, I will surely die. I cannot boast of my own strength. I am strong because I am in the body. If I am disconnected from the body, I am altogether finished; by the laying on of hands, though, I am connected to the body.

* Editor's note: not only the apostles, but also others laid hands on the believers (see Acts 9:17 and 1 Tim. 4:14).

At the time of the laying on of hands, I should realize, "Oh, Lord, I cannot live by myself; I have to confess this day that I am but one member in the body. Only in the body can I live, only in the body can I have the oil." Is this clear? One receives the oil because the Head has been anointed. If one is subject to the Head and is also joined to all the children of God, his submission as a member within the body draws the oil upon him.

Supplementary Lesson on the Laying on of Hands

Let us take up the case of the Samaritans and the case of the Ephesians. In Samaria a number of people believed in the Lord and were baptized through the labor of Philip, but they did not receive the Holy Spirit. According to God's Word, they were saved. They did not receive the Holy Spirit because they were only baptized in the name of the Lord Jesus. Now when the apostles who were in Jerusalem heard that Samaria had received the word of God, they sent Peter and John over to pray for the believers in Samaria that the latter might be given the Holy Spirit. As the apostles laid their hands on them, they received the Holy Spirit.

What is the advantage of the laying on of hands as illustrated by this particular incident? It enables the oil to flow to me. I, as a member, today acknowledge my place in the body and take my position under the Head. Such acknowledgement brings the oil upon me. A new believer can receive the anointing of the precious oil right away through the laying on of hands, even though it takes a lifetime for him to learn well all the lessons involved in it.

In baptism I declare that I have forsaken the world; in

the laying on of hands I announce that I have entered into the body. The former is negative in that I give up the world while the latter is positive in that I join the body. It means that I need this day to be identified with all the children of God, and I need to be subject to the authority of the Head. When I place my whole being under the authority of the Head, I receive the inflow of the oil. As soon as my position is right, the oil starts to flow to me. But if my position is wrong, how can the oil come to me? The Samaritans were in a peculiar situation: they had believed in the Lord and were saved; yet they had not received the Holy Spirit. The apostles came to put them under the Head. By laying hands on their heads, thus putting them under the authority of the Head and joining them to the whole body, the marvelous thing happened—the Holy Spirit was poured upon them.

Next comes the incident in Ephesus. When Paul went there to preach the gospel, he found twelve disciples who had already been baptized with the baptism of John. They were disciples, they had believed; yet they had only received the baptism of John. Paul therefore asked them if they had received the Holy Spirit when they believed. They answered negatively by saying they had not so much as heard whether the Holy Spirit had been given. Paul immediately discovered they were deficient in something fundamental.

This story is rather interesting. Why had they not received the Holy Spirit if they had already believed? The answer is that there was something lacking in the first principles. They had been baptized, but upon inquiry it was discovered that they had been baptized with the baptism of John, not baptized into Christ. Hence Paul prescribed believer's baptism for them, that they should be baptized into the name of the Lord Jesus. Once this step was taken, he laid hands on them without asking any further questions. Through the laying on of hands, they were identified with the body and were made subject to the authority of the Head.

However, no one should have the laying on of hands without first being baptized. (The house of Cornelius, though, was an exception which will later be discussed.) The rule is: the Holy Spirit descends on those who have been delivered from the world and identified with Christ in death and resurrection through baptism; they then see how they must live in the body and be subject to the authority of the Head. Let me emphatically say that the anointing oil is more than a mere outward manifestation; it is an inward reality.

Psalm 133 shows us how the Head is anointed. In the anointing of the Head, the whole body is anointed; thus every member is anointed. Immediately praises rise up in me for the oil which has flowed down from the Head and has reached me, a member of the body. Whether the Lord gives outward manifestation or not is a minor concern. The outward phenomena of Pentecost ought not to be overly stressed, for we believe it is but to affirm that these people were being anointed. The issue lies in the anointing, not in the outward manifestation. The thing that is important is to know from where the oil comes. The anointing upon the Head is what has become the anointing upon the member. For this reason, the laying on of hands with prayer is a marvelous thing.

The One Exception in the Bible

The only exception in the Bible to the above happened in the house of Cornelius. The household of Cornelius had neither been baptized nor had had the laying on of hands; nonetheless, the Holy Spirit came upon them. Why was there this one exception? Since the time of Pentecost, all the apostles originally had the idea that the grace of the Lord was only for the Jews. They themselves were Jews; even the Lord Jesus was a Jew. At Pentecost the Holy Spirit came upon the Jews. The three thousand saved then and the five thousand saved later were all Jews, Jews who had returned to Jerusalem from various nations. So up to the time of Cornelius, all who had received this grace were Jews. Whether the same grace would be given to the Gentiles was unknown to them. The Jews customarily looked down upon the Gentiles as dogs and lower animals. Even Peter found it very hard to change his view.

We all know it is not easy to break through darkened minds. It was, therefore, a matter of great significance to open the door of salvation to the Gentiles. This began with the house of Cornelius. Even in the case of the Samaritans, the people were related to the Jews, though they were not pure Jews. But the Lord also desired to save the Gentiles. How was He going to initiate this? First, He gave Peter a vision of "a certain vessel descending, as it were a great sheet, let down by four corners upon the earth: wherein were all manner of fourfooted beasts and creeping things of the earth and birds of the heaven" (Acts 10:11–12). The Lord commanded Peter to rise, kill, and eat. But Peter seemed to know better than God's command for he an-

30

swered that he had never eaten such things, meaning he had never had anything to do with Gentiles. This was done three times until Peter got the message. How very stubborn the human mind is! After three times, even people with a poor memory can remember. Peter could not pretend that he had seen wrongly nor could he excuse himself by saying he had forgotten.

As he meditated on the vision, the men from Caesarea were at the door asking for him. He immediately understood the purport of it. Even dogs under the table ate the children's crumbs; the Gentiles had their share in the salvation of God. He went with the men unhesitatingly; but, still, to baptize the household of Cornelius was something he dared not do. True, these Gentiles had already believed, but what would the brothers from Joppa accompanying him say if he baptized them? They would not recognize the baptism and would accuse Peter of acting independently. He was in a dilemma. He himself was clear as to the Lord's intention, but these brethren were not clear. So how could he make a move? But the Lord answered by pouring the Holy Spirit upon Cornelius and the other Gentiles though they had neither been baptized nor received the laying on of hands. Thus, when he returned to Jerusalem, Peter could say that since the Holy Spirit had descended before he made the gospel clear, he could do nothing but make up the deficiency by baptizing them. The baptism was for the sake of their being separated from the world and entering into Christ. The laying on of hands was omitted, however, because they already had received the anointing oil which it signified.

Later on, at the council in Jerusalem, the same problem

concerning the Gentiles was raised. Peter restated his experience, and thus the door of salvation was kept open to the Gentiles.

In Samaria there was the laying on of hands, but in Caesarea there was none. In Acts 15 the Lord used this case in Caesarea to prove Paul's point, but in Acts 19 Paul himself laid hands on the disciples he found in Ephesus. Thus it shows that the matter of the laying on of hands yet continues up to the present.

We Must Walk with All of God's Children

New believers need to be shown that they cannot live independently but they must be members one of another and learn to be subject to the authority of the Head. They ought not to be rebellious, but should rather walk together with all the children of God. Thus they will manifest the *fact* of anointing both in their lives and in their works.

ASSEMBLING TOGETHER

Not forsaking our own assembling together, as the custom of some is, but exhorting one another; and so much the more, as ye see the day drawing nigh.

Heb. 10:25

For where two or three are gathered together in my name, there am I in the midst of them.

Matt. 18:20

And they continued stedfastly in the apostles' teaching and fellowship, in the breaking of bread and the prayers.

Acts 2:42

If therefore the whole church be assembled together . . .

1 Cor. 14:23

What is it then, brethren? When ye come together, each one hath a psalm, hath a teaching, hath a revelation, hath a tongue, hath an interpretation. Let all things be done unto edifying.

1 Cor. 14:26

God Gives Grace in the Assembly

The Word of God exhorts us not to forsake assembling together. Why? Because God's grace to men is of two

33

kinds: personal and corporate. If being a Christian were only a personal matter, one could stay home and personally receive grace from God. But God gives corporate grace as well as personal grace, and this corporate grace can only be obtained in the assembly.

Many prayers can be offered privately. God answers if one prays with faith and doubts not. However, there is another kind of prayer, and this kind must be offered in the assembly if it is to be heard. It must be prayed in the name of the Lord by two or more people. God's corporate grace is only granted in the assembly; it is not given to individuals as such. Many big issues having wide effects can never be solved unless people pray together in the meeting. So we can see that God answers two kinds of prayer: private prayer and corporate prayer. If people do not assemble together, some prayers will be left unanswered.

The same is true with the study of God's Word. We have said before that as we open the Bible we expect God to shed light upon us. Indeed, in reading the Bible we are granted grace to understand. Nevertheless, certain Scriptures will not be opened up to us except in the gathering of the saints. They cannot be understood individually; but in the meeting special grace is given to understand them.

Many of God's workers can testify that the Scriptures they come to know in the meetings are just as full of light as those God unfolds to them in private. Frequently in the meetings God leads from one word to another word. Light reflects from one person to another so that the degree of light is increased. Thus we receive corporate grace. Were we to forsake assembling together, the most we would get would be personal grace. What a great amount of corporate grace we then would forfeit.

Christianity is Collective

Let us further remember that Christianity is unique in that it is not individual but collective in nature. It stresses the assembling together of the saints. All other religions advocate individual piety; Christianity alone calls people to assemble. God's special grace falls on the gathering of believers.

Because of this, the Word of God commands us not to forsake assembling together. Even in the Old Testament, God ordained that the Jews should assemble; then He called them the congregation of the Lord. To be a congregation they had to assemble together. Thus in the Old Testament God already emphasized the gathering of His people. In the New Testament it becomes much clearer that men ought to assemble in order that they may receive His grace. The command of the Bible is, "not forsaking our own assembling together." No one can forsake such assembling without forfeiting grace. It is foolish to cease gathering with the saints.

The Bible records many occasions of assembling together. While our Lord was on earth, He often met with His disciples. Though sometimes He conversed with them individually, yet He was more interested in gathering together with them. He gathered with them in boats, in homes, on top of mountains, and even inside a borrowed upper room on the night of His betrayal. After His resurrection, He met with them behind a closed door. Before the day of Pentecost, the disciples gathered with one accord and continued steadfastly in prayer. On the day of Pentecost, they were also all together in one place. Again, in Acts 2, we find that all who received the word and were baptized "continued stedfastly in the apostles' teaching and fellowship, in the breaking of bread and the prayers" (Acts 2:42). Later on, under persecution, they went to their own company where there was a gathering for prayer. When Peter was miraculously released from prison, he too went to a home where the people assembled in prayer. The epistles also command believers to not forsake assembling together. In Corinthians, special mention is made of the whole church coming together. No one who belongs to the church ought to keep himself away from such gatherings.

What is the meaning of the word "church" (more accurately, "assembly") in Greek? *Ek* means "out of," and *klesis* means "a calling." *Ecclesia* means "the called-out ones assembled." Today God has not only called out a people but He also wants them to assemble together. If each one who is called were to maintain his independence, there would be no church. Thus we are shown the importance of assembling together.

The Body Is Related to the Assembly

We all know that both chapters 12 and 14 of 1 Corinthians speak of the gifts of the Holy Spirit. The distinction between these two chapters is that, whereas in chapter 12 it speaks of gifts in the body, in chapter 14 it is gifts in the gathering. In reading these two chapters together, it is evident that the body in chapter 12 is functioning in chapter 14. The gifts in the body are especially manifested in the meetings. The body functions coordinately: the eyes help the feet, the ears the hands, and the hands the mouth. These members affect and sustain one another; their functioning is most noticeable in the gatherings. Hence, those who rarely meet have little chance to know what the functioning of the body means. Due to the interaction of one member with another, our prayers in the meetings are more easily heard by God and we also receive more light. What we see privately does not exceed what we see in the meetings, because all the ministries which God has set in the church are manifested in the times of gathering. God has appointed these ministries for the sake of the saints assembled together.

God's light is in the Holy of Holies. In the outer court there is the light of the sun. The Holy Place is naturally dark, because it does not have the sunlight. It is lit, however, by the lamp containing olive oil. In the Holy of Holies, there is neither natural light nor artificial light but only the light of God. God's light does not dwell in the Holy Place but in the Holy of Holies. For anyone to see this light, he has to be in the Holy of Holies. When one is alone, he may receive some light, but this cannot be reckoned as being in the Holy of Holies. Only when the saints are assembled together does the church become God's dwelling place, and then God's light shines in full splendor. The time the church gathers is the time God manifests His light. We do not know why; we can only say that at this time there is the mutual working of the members of the body which enables God to show forth His light.

New believers may not understand what this light of the body is. They probably do not pay much attention to meetings and thus they miss the light of the sanctuary. Many basic spiritual workings are in the body. By meeting often we may learn much through the operation of these workings. So let us then, joyfully gather together.

It is recorded in the Old Testament that "one (shall) chase a thousand, and two put ten thousand to flight" (Deut. 32:30). We do not know how this is possible, but we do know it is a fact. Naturally speaking, if one can chase a thousand, then two will chase two thousand. Yet God says two will chase ten thousand—an additional eight thousand! This addition is the surplus which is found in meeting together. Let us therefore not be content with personal grace but rather seek to gain corporate grace.

The Lord's Presence Is in the Gathering

Furthermore, the Lord twice promises us His special presence: once in Matthew 18 and once in Matthew 28. The latter, "Lo, I am with you always, even unto the end of the world," pertains to witnessing for Christ; the former, "for where two or three are gathered together in my name, there am I in the midst of them," pertains to meeting in His name. These two promises of His presence are different from the presence of the Lord with us personally.

Many only know His presence in a personal way, but such knowledge is insufficient. His most powerful and overwhelming presence is known only in the meeting. Although there is His presence with you personally, it is bound to be of a lesser degree. Only in assembling together with brothers and sisters do you experience His presence in a way that you never did before. Learn, therefore, to know this presence in the meetings. It is a tremendous grace which cannot be otherwise obtained.

How wonderful the assembling of God's children is! We do not know how the body operates, but we do know that it does function. As one brother rises, you see light. When another brother stands up, you sense the presence of the Lord. Still another brother opens his mouth to pray, and you touch God. Yet another says a few words, and you receive the supply of life. Let me tell you, this is something beyond explanation—how the body of Christ works together. We will not understand until we stand before the Lord at His return. Today we can only follow that which the Lord has ordained.

How We Should Assemble

How should we gather? The Bible lays down a basic principle: all gatherings must be in the name of the Lord. The meaning of this is simply that we gather under the authority of the Lord and also are centered upon Him. Our purpose in coming together is to meet with the Lord, for our attraction is to Him. Let it be clear that we do not go to the meetings to see certain brothers or sisters, for our attraction to the meeting is not them. The Lord is the center. We go, along with many other brothers and sisters, to appear before Him.

Why is it that we gather in the name of the Lord? Because, physically speaking, the Lord is not here. Were He physically present, His name would not be so prominent. But since He is absent, His name becomes more noticeable. Today our Lord is physically in heaven, yet He has left a name on earth. So today we gather in His name that we may draw nigh to Him. He promises us that if we do so gather, He will be in our midst: that is, His Spirit will be in the midst of our gathering.

When we assemble, we do not go to hear a preacher but rather to meet the Lord. This is a concept that must be firmly established within us. Should we meet in order to hear a certain man, are we not gathering in this man's name and not in the name of our Lord? Many advertise the names of speakers in the newspaper; unknowingly they are asking people to gather around these men.

Although our Lord is in heaven, He is yet among us because His name is in our midst and so is His Spirit. The Holy Spirit is the custodian of the Lord's name. He is sent to protect and look after the Lord's name. He is here to exalt that name which is above all names. We must, therefore, gather unto the name of the Lord.

Another principle which governs a gathering is the edifying or building up of God's people. According to 1 Corinthians 14, this is a purpose found in all the gatherings—that others, not ourselves, may be edified. Paul explains how speaking in a tongue edifies oneself but that it needs interpretation so that others may receive help. If there is no interpretation, the one with the tongue should keep silent in the church. In other words, the principle of speaking in a tongue is for self-edification and not for the edifying of others, whereas that of interpretation is to impart what one has to others for their edification. That which only edifies self and not others should not be expressed in the meeting.

Therefore, when we come to the meeting, we need to consider whether or not others will be edified. Even asking questions is not merely for our personal benefit. In whatever I do, do I help the meeting or do I damage it? The place where individualism is manifested most is in the meetings. Some people can only think of themselves. If they have a hymn they want to sing, they try their best to get it in. Indeed, they themselves may be edified, but is the meeting helped?

Do remember that both our speaking and our silence may hurt others. If we are not considerate of others, we will cause the meeting to suffer loss. Whether we speak or remain silent, it is to profit the meeting by edifying the people. Do not refrain from speaking when your speaking is needed. All things should be done for edification.

In many places there are difficulties because young believers are not trained in this respect. They are like horses let loose, running all around the place. Under those conditions, how can we expect a good meeting? The responsible brothers must hold the reins if the gathering is to be profitable.

Finally, we wish to repeat that all who gather should have one aim: the edification of one another, not of oneself. I should refrain from doing anything that may hinder others. If my not speaking may inhibit others, then I will speak. In all things I must learn to edify others.

Alas, many have been Christians for years yet still do not know how to meet. They care for nobody but themselves. They respect neither the Lord nor the Holy Spirit. They think they are the meeting. They alone are present in the meeting. May young believers learn from this. Never come to the meeting with the thought of what you can get; rather let all your actions be for the benefit of others. If speaking is good for others, then speak; if silence is better, then keep quiet. The basic principle of a meeting is edification of the people.

One should not speak in the meeting so as to gratify himself. Though he may be satisfied, a hundred others may be disturbed. He may feel burdened if he does not speak, but his brethren will have to take his burden back home with them if he does speak. If one person speaks out of order, the whole assembly suffers. Let me state emphatically: the Holy Spirit should not be offended in the meeting. If He is offended, the spiritual blessing will be lost. When we are concerned with others' needs and others' edification, then the Holy Spirit is honored and He will do the work of edification both in us and in others.

Be a humble soul from the very start. If anyone is uncertain whether his speaking edifies or not, it is best for him to consult with the responsible brothers, to ask them, "Brothers, do you think I should speak more or speak less in the meetings?" Be humble and do not think too highly of yourself, as if you were the marvel of these twenty centuries—the best singer and the best preacher! Let us learn humility that our gatherings may be strong. Whenever people walk into our midst, they should instantly sense the presence of God. This is the work of the Holy Spirit. It will cause them to fall down on their faces and worship God, declaring that God is indeed among us.

VARIOUS MEETINGS

In the previous lesson we stated the principle of meeting together; now we will turn to its practice. From what I personally can see, there are five different types of meetings in the Bible. They are gospel meetings, breaking of bread meetings, prayer meetings, exercise of gifts or fellowship meetings, and ministry or preaching meetings. We can find examples of all these in the Bible. Thus we know that at the time of the apostles in the New Testament days, there were at least these five different types of meetings. The church today also needs to have all these various meetings if it is to be strong before God. We must learn how to meet in order to help brothers and sisters grow in the Lord.

Gospel Meetings

The most important meeting in the New Testament is the gospel meeting. It is the first type of meeting in the book of Acts as well as in the Gospels. Judging from the history of the early church, gospel meetings were the most basic of all the church meetings.

It was not till after the church began to degenerate during the third and fourth centuries that gospel meetings gradually lost their prominence and ministry meetings took on the leading role. The popularity of listening to sermons is a reflection on the weakened condition of the church. In the early church, preaching the gospel rather than listening to sermons occupied the foremost place. Today's reverse situation is a proof of the failure of the church. To have a strong church, the preaching of the gospel should be restored to its original position of being the most basic of all the meetings.

Brothers and sisters everywhere need to receive light from God and not imitate the ways of traditional Christianity. Christianity generally emphasizes sermons; we have unconsciously followed that practice. May the Lord be gracious to us so that we may be recovered to the original state of the church.

The Lord has put the church on the earth not only for the purpose of building herself up but also for the sake of gathering in souls to be material for the church. The gift of evangelist does not head the list so far as the inward upbuilding of the church is concerned, but when the gospel was preached in Acts, evangelism was the first gift to be exercised. Philip's evangelization of Samaria in Acts 8 is a clear evidence of this. During the time of the expansion of the church of God, the gift of evangelist occupied the first and foremost place. Let us therefore correct the custom of traditional Christianity which makes listening to sermons the center of all gatherings; let us put gospel meetings back again in their proper place.

As soon as people come to believe in the Lord, they should immediately start to help in the preaching of the gospel. Do not allow them to develop the habit of listening to sermons; instead, help them to cultivate the habit of serving by preaching the gospel. There should be at least one gospel meeting every week. Set aside the best time for this meeting, either the Lord's day morning or the Lord's day afternoon. Arrange for two or three young believers who are somewhat more advanced and gifted to give their testimonies or to preach the gospel. The older ones either can help these younger ones or, upon occasion, preach themselves. Do, however, give the young ones opportunity. There should be no more than three giving testimonies or preaching the gospel lest the meeting become confusing. The best is to have three persons.

1. Come to Cooperate

New believers attending the gospel meetings should realize that the message is not for them but for the unbelievers. Therefore, no believer should come with a critical or indifferent or uncooperative attitude. Do not judge in your hearts whether the gospel is preached well or not. Remember, God has not arranged the meeting for you to hear the gospel. Your attitude should be that of desiring that souls may be saved. You come to cooperate, not to criticize.

2. Come as the Body

Encourage all the brothers and sisters to attend the gospel meetings. Never let any brothers and sisters think they do not need to attend because they are already saved.

True, you are saved, but in the gospel meetings you have work to do. Do not come passively, but rather come in order to work. Let no one be careless about the gospel meetings. The question does not lie in whether or not you know the gospel. Indeed, you should know the substance of every meeting. But you come to the gospel meetings so that you can help, thus having a part in it yourself.

3. BRING A FRIEND

One thing we must certainly do is bring people to the gospel meetings. Before the meeting time, we should invite our friends and relatives. We should extend our invitation to them several days in advance. We should not come to the gospel meeting alone but should at least have one person with us. Do not bring more than four with you, for if you bring too many you will not be able to take care of them. Should it be, though, that God gives you grace to bring in ten, twenty, thirty people, what should you do? You should ask for help from other brothers and sisters. However, do not bring in more unbelievers than you can handle.

It is clear, then, that when you attend gospel meetings, you do not just arrive on time. Those who attend the meetings must prepare beforehand by inviting friends. As the time for the meeting draws close, you should bring your friend in or, as Luke says: Go out into the streets and lanes of the city, yes, even to the highways and byways, and compel the people to come in (See Lk. 14:21-23). You do have a responsibility in the preaching of the gospel. You should at least bring in another soul. How can a gospel meeting be held if only believers attend? Make all the arrangements in advance. Tell the people whom you have invited where you will meet them. It is absolutely necessary that you bring people in.

4. TAKE CARE OF THE FRIEND

There are several things we should do during the meeting to take care of the friends whom we bring.

SIT NEXT TO THE FRIENDS

When an unbeliever comes to the meeting, he has no idea where to sit. It depends entirely upon you. If there are ushers in the meeting, you should ask them where you should seat your friend. You should follow their directions. If you bring in one person, sit next to him; if two people, sit in the middle; if four, put two on each side of you. Do not try to take care of more than four, for this will be an impossibility. If you have more than four to bring, you should prearrange to have some other brothers and sisters take care of them. Seating is quite important in a gospel meeting. Do not fill the hall with unbelievers. Let the believers and the unbelievers sit next to each other.

HELP FIND BIBLE VERSES AND EXPLAIN TERMINOLOGY

After you have been seated, you have quite a few things to do. You should help unbelievers find the Bible verses given by the preacher. Suppose the preacher speaks on Joshua; you must find the place in the Bible for your friend, for he does not know where Joshua is. If the preacher uses a special term without explaining it, then you should softly whisper to your friend the meaning of the term. If he seems puzzled by names of persons and places, you can tell him that these are Bible names. You need to supplement whatever lack there is in the preaching. Do not speak too loudly, but whisper clearly enough to make him understand. Mr. Paget Wilkes mentioned an incident in one of his books. Once a preacher from England went to Japan to preach the gospel. Many came to hear him. His first sentence was: "You know the story of the exodus of the people of Israel out of Egypt." Mr. Wilkes immediately went to him and said, "These people know nothing of the Israelites nor of Egypt." Such a move was very wise for it would have taken at least an hour to explain who the Israelites were, what Egypt was, and how the Israelites came out of Egypt. The preacher did not know that these people were so ignorant. However, had he continued without an explanation, then those near the unbelievers could simply have whispered, "The Israelites were Jews, Egypt was a nation, and the Israelites were freed from slavery when they came out of Egypt."

FIND THE HYMNS

You should also help the unbelievers to find the hymns. Instruct them especially when a chorus is sung. If you have four friends with you, it will be all you can do to take care of them in this matter.

OBSERVE REACTIONS AND PRAY

Observe carefully the reaction of the unbelievers as they listen. If their reaction is negative, pray that the Lord will soften their hearts. If you feel a particular person is proud, ask the Lord to break down his pride. Whether the church preaches the gospel well or not depends on how the gospel meeting is conducted. Unless the whole body is mobilized and all the brothers and sisters are involved, there is no way to preach the gospel. You are the one who knows those whom you have brought in. It is you who should ob-serve them and pray: "Lord, move his heart. Lord, give him understanding. Lord, break down his pride that he may hear." Sometimes you may feel it would be good if the one preaching would say certain words. If so, you may pray thus: "Lord, for the sake of a particular need, make the preacher say those words." Often you will find that the preacher comes out with just those words. Thus, through prayer, you take care of your friends.

HELP THE FRIENDS TO ACCEPT THE LORD

The most important part is to help your friend accept the Lord once you find he is evidently moved. Send the word of the Lord into his heart through prayer. Ask the Lord to make him hear, to let His word sink into his heart, and to enlighten him with the word.

When the preacher is ready to draw in the net, you should encourage your friend by saying, "You too are a sinner. I hope you will accept the Lord." If you notice he is wavering between two opinions, give him a push in the right direction. Do not allow Satan to set up an obstacle or to pull him away. You should work as soon as you perceive that he is somewhat moved. Say to him, "Believe and accept the Lord now. Refusal may mean eternal suffering." When you talk to him, your manner should be serious and sober, lest through frivolity and jesting you lose your effectiveness. When the preacher urges people to accept the Lord, you should help. It is a disgrace if we do not take care of the people for whose salvation we are working while at the same time Satan is diligently working for their perdition. As Satan carefully guards his possessions, so should we attentively watch over those under our care. We must help them to be saved.

Remember a basic principle: save a person by all possible means. D. L. Moody once said that if we wrongly lead a person to the Lord, God will forgive us. Let our eyes be open. Whether by pushing or by pulling, let us bring people to the Lord. Let us not rest until they are saved.

HELP THEM TO SIGN THEIR NAMES

During the closing of the meeting, help them to sign their names. Some people may be afraid to write down their names, asking why they should do so. You can explain to them that it is for the purpose of visitation.

HELP THEM TO PRAY

Your work is not yet finished. Finally, at the time of prayer, you should help them to pray with you or with another brother or sister. You must not leave anything undone.

VISIT THEM WITH ANOTHER CHRISTIAN

When the church sends people to visit those who have signed their names, you should go with them to visit those whom you have contacted. You may have to go not just once, but two or three times until that soul is saved.

In conclusion, gospel meetings should be the first of all the meetings. The whole body of brothers and sisters must understand its significance and participate in the work. This is how the church will grow and become stronger. May God do the work of recovery in our midst. May the gospel meetings be the first of all the meetings as they were in the New Testament. In this meeting, every brother and sister must actively work; no one should be lax. Let me tell you, if you get all the new believers to start working for the Lord during the first year of their regeneration, you will make it impossible for them to just sit and listen passively to sermons afterward. If you do this, then the church will truly be in a good condition. The gospel meetings will become a workshop for all the brothers and sisters. Whether a person can preach is not the question; the task is for us to save souls. If we all understand what the gospel meeting is, then there will also always be the need for pulpit ministry. That, however, is not the aim; nowhere in the New Testament does God wish us to aim for that. It is the practice of today's Christianity, but not the practice in the Bible.

Breaking of Bread Meetings

The next important meeting is that of the breaking of bread.

1. THE TABLE AND THE SUPPER

According to the Word of God, the meeting for the breaking of bread has two different aspects: one is the Lord's table and the other is the Lord's supper. 1 Corinthians 10 refers to the Lord's table while 1 Corinthians 11 points to the Lord's supper. However, we would like to consider them in reverse order, starting with 1 Corinthians 11. In the Lord's supper, the bread is the Lord's body, alluding to the physical body of the Lord. By partaking of this body which is given for the remission of our sins, we may thus receive life. So the basic thought of the Lord's supper is to remember the Lord. The meaning of the

Lord's supper lies in remembering how the Lord shed His blood in order that our sins might be forgiven.

But 1 Corinthians 10 takes up another aspect. The breaking of bread is called the Lord's table. "Seeing that we, who are many, are one bread" (v. 17). The bread in 1 Corinthians 11 is the physical body of the Lord but in 1 Corinthians 10 it is us. We who are many are one bread. In other words, the Lord's table emphasizes the communion or fellowship of God's children. Chapter 11 stresses remembering the Lord, while chapter 10 stresses the fellowship of the children of God.

Hence, we have two meanings: one is direct, our focus turned heavenward, remembering the Lord; the other focuses on having fellowship with one another, the one bread on the table. We all have part in this bread; we are all people of this one bread. You belong to this bread; so do I. You have accepted the Savior; so have I. Therefore we ought to have fellowship in the Lord. At the breaking of bread, we come before the Lord both to have fellowship with Him and with all His children.

2. TWO SECTIONS—THE LORD'S AND THE FATHER'S

There is something else to be noticed: the meeting for the breaking of bread is divided into two sections. Let us explain.

Since salvation is composed of two aspects, the breaking of bread meeting naturally follows suit. The first aspect of salvation is that I see myself as a sinner condemned to die, but, through the mercy of the Lord who came to the world and died for me, I have my sins forgiven by accepting the blood of the Lord Jesus. Salvation does not stop at this point, though. After being saved and belonging to the

Lord, I am brought by the Lord Jesus to God whom He calls His Father and my Father. The Holy Spirit who dwells in me causes me to call God, "Abba, Father." This is the second aspect of salvation. In other words, salvation consists of two aspects: the first is the Lord's, and the second is the Father's. The first aspect pertains to forgiveness while the second aspect pertains to acceptance. These two aspects should not be confused in salvation. First I receive forgiveness; then I am accepted before God. As a sinner, I must be connected to the Lord before I can be related to God.

Hence the Bible tells us, "Whosoever denieth the Son, the same hath not the Father: he that confesseth the Son hath the Father also" (1 John 2:23). Salvation has both the Son's side, the Lord's aspect, and the Father's side, God's aspect. No one can bypass the Son and come to the Father. He must first come to the Son, to the cross, in order to receive forgiveness, for the just has died for the unjust. Then the Son will lead him to the Father. So, it is first forgiveness and afterwards acceptance. We need to be very clear on this point.

Due to these two aspects of salvation, the meeting for the breaking of bread as a remembrance of salvation naturally falls into two sections. Before the breaking of the bread is the section for the Son; after the bread is broken it becomes the section for the Father. The first portion is the Lord's; the second portion is God's.

FIRST COME TO THE LORD

As we come first to the Lord, we realize what great sinners we are, how we are children of rebellion and of wrath, under the judgment of God without any means of saving

53

ourselves. But, thank God, through the Lord Jesus who shed His blood for the remission of our sins, we may come to Him today to receive His life. So in the first section, all our prayers and hymns and praises should be directed to the Lord. We as sinners first draw nigh to the Lord to have our sins forgiven.

If we go to the temple, the first thing we meet is the altar, not the ark. Later on, we reach the ark, but first we arrive at the altar. Since the altar is a type of the cross, we first of all approach the Lord with thanksgiving and praise.

In the presence of the Lord, we offer our thanks and praise. Indeed, we can do nothing else but thank and praise Him, for before the blood there is no need to ask for anything. It is inappropriate to ask for things at this meeting. We cannot ask the Lord to shed His blood for us; He has already done that. So we need not ask. All we can do is to thank and praise Him. Whether it is in the form of prayer or in the form of a hymn, nonetheless it is thanks and praise. In thanksgiving, we notice the Lord's work; in praising we consider the Lord Himself. We thank Him for what He has done; and we praise Him for what He is.

In the beginning there may be more thanks; gradually, though, thanks will give way to praise. We thank and we praise. What a wonderful work He has done for us, and what a wonderful Savior He is in His person and position. When our thanks and praises reach a peak, the time to break the bread has arrived. The whole assembly is now brought to the Lord.

THEN THE FATHER ACCEPTS US

After the bread is broken, the second section of the meeting begins. The Lord does not desire that we come to

Him and stop there. He wants us to go on to the Father. Is it not wonderful that it is we who accept the Lord, but it is the Father who accepts us? We must be clear on this point. According to the truth of the gospel, we accept the Lord, not the Father. Nowhere in the Bible are we exhorted to receive the Father, for it is always the Son on whom we are called to believe. The Father receives us *after* we have become acceptable in His Son. Our accepting the Son is but half of salvation; the Father's accepting us is the other half. Consequently, after the bread is broken, we should come to the Father. We should begin to praise God the Father.

On the morning of His resurrection, the Lord told Mary, "I ascend unto my Father and your Father, and my God and your God" (John 20:17b). Before His resurrection, He always said, "My Father," but after His death and resurrection, His Father became our Father also. So in the second section of the meeting for the breaking of bread, the Lord leads us to the Father. Brothers and sisters, He who leads us in the meeting is the Holy Spirit, and the leading of the Holy Spirit is not contradictory to the principle of salvation. The Holy Spirit will lead us first to the Son and then to the Father. Let us learn to follow His leading and go to the Father after having broken the bread.

Of the three parables recorded in Luke 15, we meet the shepherd in the first and the Father in the last. First the good shepherd, then the good Father. The good shepherd comes out to seek us, but the good Father waits at home for us to find Him. The good shepherd leaves home, but the good Father stays at home to receive us. In the first part of the worship meeting, we meet the good shepherd; so afterwards we come to approach the Father. For this reason, all the hymns and prayers in the second part are centered on the Father. We do not follow our own dictates but are so led by the Holy Spirit. I believe if the Holy Spirit has His free way with us, He will undoubtedly lead us in this manner.

THE SON LEADS MANY SONS IN PRAISE

In Hebrews 2 we notice a marvelous thing: the Lord Jesus brings many sons into glory. The Lord Jesus as the first-born Son leads many sons into glory. While He was on earth, He was God's only begotten Son, because He was the only Son God had. But after His death and resurrection, He transformed us into many sons. We do not become sons until after we have met the Lord Jesus. Thus it is that in the second part of the breaking of bread, the meeting takes up the character of the first-born Son leading many sons. "In the midst of the congregation will I sing thy praise" (Heb. 2:12b). This is the time when the first-born Son leads many sons in praise of the Father. How precious it is that not only the many sons may come to the Father but that it is the first-born who leads the many sons to the Father to praise His holy name. Let us learn to rise up high in our spirit.

The throne of God is established on praises. When the church of God starts to praise, she begins to touch the throne. The more we learn to praise, the more we know the throne.

The type of meeting in Hebrews 2 is the best of all meetings. May we begin to learn a little today. One day in heaven we shall meet in a perfect manner. Nevertheless, let us begin to practice what is meant by being led of the first-born Son to sing praise to the Father in the congregation in these days before we enter into glory. Let me tell you, this is the ultimate of all the church meetings. It is really glorious.

Prayer Meetings

The prayer meeting is also an important meeting. Each kind of meeting has its own particular characteristic. The testimony which God intends us to maintain on earth is to be fulfilled jointly by preaching the gospel, breaking bread, and praying together. Prayer meetings can be both difficult and easy. New believers need to learn about this kind of meeting.

1. WITH ONE ACCORD

A fundamental requirement for brothers and sisters praying together is to be of one accord. The Lord tells us in Matthew 18 that we must agree on earth. Before and on the day of Pentecost, the one hundred and twenty believers prayed with one accord (Acts 4:1-2). Therefore, the first condition of a prayer meeting is to be of one heart and one mind. How can people gather for prayer if each one has his own mind? The word "agree" in Matthew is most weighty. The Lord promises that, "If two of you shall agree on earth as touching anything that they shall ask, it shall be done for them. . . ." (v. 19). This particular word in Greek is used in music to denote harmony. If a person is playing alone, there is no problem. But if three play together, one the piano, one the violin, and one the flute, should one of them play out of tune, the result is discord. Likewise our prayers should not be out of harmony. If we are able to agree with one another, God will hear whatever we ask. What we bind on earth shall be bound in heaven, and what we loose on earth shall be loosed in heaven. The basic condition is harmony. Therefore let us learn to be harmonious and not to pray each according to his own wish.

2. WITH SPECIFIC REQUESTS

How can we achieve this goal of harmony? I observe that the greatest problem in many prayer meetings lies in too many requests. As long as there are too many subjects for which to pray, it is very difficult to arrive at harmony. We ourselves create disunity by having fifty or sixty prayer items. It becomes an all-inclusive meeting. We do not find such a situation in the Bible. What we do find there is praying for a specific matter. For example, the church prayed for Peter while he was in prison. We too should not pray for many things, but pray rather for one specific matter. It is easy to achieve agreement when there is only one topic. Too many items will make our prayers like a routine.

I believe the prayer meetings in many places require a drastic change. Let each prayer meeting be for just one thing. Perhaps we should pray for the unemployed brothers and sisters or for the sick or for the poor—one of these and nothing else. With one subject we can readily agree.

If there is yet time after we have finished praying for one matter, then we may mention another matter for prayer. We must do the work of prayer before God. The prayer meeting may be divided into two parts, in each part praying for one thing. To pray for two things at the same time makes it difficult for people to be of one accord. Do not therefore carelessly announce two items for prayer at the commencement. Let the responsible brother announce one thing at a time. I think the greatest need in a prayer meeting is to make the requests simple. The aim of prayer is to accomplish things, to get things done. It is not for social reasons or to please people; thus it cannot include everything.

The power of the specific prayer uttered in Acts 1 and 2 produced Pentecost. As the cross was the work accomplished by the Son of God, so Pentecost was the work accomplished through the prayer of God's children. How was it done? By praying with one accord. Let us, too, pray in that concentrated, not scattered, manner.

Everyone who attends a prayer meeting should come with the preparation of faith. If possible, the brothers and sisters should be told beforehand of the prayer request so that they may have a burden for it. First the sensing of the need, then the burden, and finally the asking.

3. In Reality

There is another basic need for the prayers at a prayer meeting, and that is, reality, or genuineness. According to my personal observation (I dare not exaggerate), I have reason to judge that one half of all the words uttered in a prayer meeting are false. The motive of many prayers is not that God may hear, but that man may approve. Whether God answers my prayer is not so important as long as it pleases men. As a consequence, prayers at the prayer meeting become pretentious and empty.

True prayer comes from the desire of the heart, not from the imagination of the mind. It expresses the feeling of the heart, so it arises from a deep longing within. For this reason prayer in the Old Testament was offered to God as incense. All Old Testament incense was made from trees. After the bark was cut, the tree oozed a kind of resin from which incense was manufactured. Hence prayer is not offering anything that might be at hand; it is the presenting of something dug out of the innermost heart. It resembles something that oozes out of wounds. Such prayers are quite different from the easygoing ones that many offer— prayers good to listen to but very ordinary in content. Let us remember well that our prayers are for God to hear, not for pleasing the ears of brothers and sisters.

If the prayers of the prayer meetings lack reality, we frankly cannot expect the church to be strong. For the church to be strong, the prayer meetings must be strong. For the prayer meetings to be strong, all the prayers must be real. We cannot afford to let them be false, for God will never reward falsehood.

Prayer is not preaching, nor is it lecturing. It is asking before God. Therefore, do not use many words as if God were ignorant of the situation and in need of your detailed intelligence reports and arguments!

We pray because we have need; we pray because we have weakness. We come to receive spiritual supply and power. According to our sense of the measure of our need, to that extent do we pray in reality. If we sense no need, our prayer is bound to be unreal.

One of the fundamental causes of feigned prayer is that the one who prays simply cannot forget the other people present. Being always conscious of people, he easily becomes insincere in his prayer. Hence in a prayer meeting, he should remember that though on the one hand his prayer does represent the whole assembly, yet on the other hand he is alone with God, asking truly according to need.

The more definite the need, the more certain the prayer. You may remember the parable used by the Lord Jesus: a friend unexpectedly arrives and you have nothing to serve him. So you go to another friend to ask for bread. The need is very definite. "Ask, and it shall be given you; seek, and ye shall find; knock, and it shall be opened unto you," says the Lord Jesus (Matt. 7:7). You dare not be careless when there is a real need. The Lord promises that if you ask, you shall have it.

4. WITH CONCISENESS

Prayer needs to be concise as well as real. Almost all the prayers in the Bible are very concise. The so-called Lord's Prayer in Matthew 6 is quite short. The Lord's own prayer before His departure, recorded in John 17, seems to be long; yet it is much shorter than the prayers of many of God's children today. Even the prayer of the whole church found in Acts 4 is concise. The prayer in Ephesians 1 is a most important prayer, but it can easily be finished in less than five minutes.

Many times the longer the prayers are, the more pretentious and empty they become. Only two sentences are real; the rest are all added. Those two sentences are for God to hear; all the rest are for the ears of brothers and sisters. We should instruct young believers to pray briefly, telling them that if the older ones pray their long prayers, it is all right, but the young ones should not do so. As a matter of fact, long prayers can cause great damage to the church.

Once, when a sister prayed on and on, exhausting the patience of the whole assembly, Moody did a very wise thing by standing up and saying, "While our sister continues her prayer, let us sing a hymn." May none of us think that we can be careless during prayer meetings. If we really pray with one accord, unbelievers who happen to come in will have to acknowledge that these Christians do have something. Long prayers dissipate strength whereas concise prayers add strength to the meeting.

The writer of the *Notes on the Pentateuch*, C. H. M., spoke well when he said to please not use your prayer to ill-treat God's children. Many may not whip you with whips, but they beat you with prayers. You can hardly remain in your seat. Let God's children pray truly and concisely.

5. WITHIN THE LIMITS OF YOUR PRIVATE PRAYERS

In corporate prayers, another basic principle to practice is to never let your public prayers exceed your private prayers. This is a good rule. As you pray in private, so pray in public. Of course, you may have to adjust your prayers to suit the public, for you cannot pray in public exactly the same way as you pray in private. This is understandable. But still, your prayers in public should not exceed your prayers in private. As a matter of fact, very few private prayers are false even though equally few public prayers are true. When you come to pray with others, you tend to say what you would not say while alone. Thus you add words to your prayers.

Though public prayer is difficult and tends to be false and long and men-pleasing, yet prayers in the prayer meetings are stronger than private prayers so far as accomplishing things is concerned. God can answer the prayers of the church far more than He can answer personal prayers. The problem today, though, is that there are more answers to personal prayers than to corporate prayers. Why is it so? Because there is so much falsehood, confusion, vain words in corporate prayers. How God would delight to answer the prayers of His children if they prayed together with simplicity and with one accord!

Exercise of Gifts Meetings

The gifts found in each local church are different. To some local churches, God may give words of revelation as well as gifts of prophecy and of teaching; to others, He may add the gift of tongues and the gift of interpreting tongues. In some places, He may give only the gift of teaching without giving any miraculous gifts; or it could be just the opposite, there being miraculous gifts without the gift of the word. We cannot dictate what God will do in His church. But what we do know is the principle of such meetings: God wishes His children to exercise their gifts. It is evident that we cannot exercise the gifts which we do not have but that we can use the gifts we do possess. Hence, no local church can imitate other local churches in this matter of exercising gifts. Each church must exercise before God whatever gifts the local brothers and sisters have. What we are describing here are meetings according to the principle of 1 Corinthians 14.

At such meetings for the exercise of gifts there may even be questions asked, for we seek to build up one another by finding light from God. So the apostle says, "When ye come together, each one hath a psalm, hath a teaching, hath a revelation, hath a tongue, hath an interpretation" (1 Cor. 14:26). If there is prophecy, let it be at the most three.

In such meetings, if there is no interpretation, let there be no speaking in tongues. Speaking in tongues is for personal edification, while tongues with interpretation is equivalent to prophesying. Tongues without interpretation does not edify the church because it has no effect on the understanding. For this reason, Paul forbids speaking in tongues in the meeting unless there is interpretation. He does not prohibit speaking in tongues, only speaking in tongues without interpretation in the meeting.

1. Do Not Be Passive

In this kind of meeting, all brothers who have the gift of the word should learn not to be passive. Often in these gift-exercising or so-called fellowship meetings, the brothers who are gifted to be ministers of God's Word assume a passive position, standing aside and letting other brothers speak. This is not right.

One thing new believers ought to know: not everyone may speak in the meetings for the exercising of gifts. Only those who have gifts may speak. We do not approve of a one-man ministry, neither do we sponsor an every-man ministry. God judges both the one-man ministry and the every-man ministry as wrong. Only the gifted should supply the word; not everyone can speak. Where does the difficulty lie today? The problem is that brothers with ministry adopt an attitude that the meeting is open to every brother, whereas in actuality it is open only to those brothers gifted in ministry, not to every brother and sister. They who are mouths refuse to speak while expecting the hands, the feet, and the ears to speak! What can you expect in such a meeting but confusion? Therefore, all the brothers who are gifted should open their mouths in the meeting. As to the rest, let them speak only when they have something of value to say.

2. Discover New Gifts

When new believers come to this meeting, they find it rather hard for they do not know what their gifts are. Since they are so young in the faith, they cannot be considered as being ministers of the word. How, then, are they to be helped? My hope is that the more advanced brothers will give these young brothers opportunity to speak. Do not seal their mouths, but advise them to speak simply and briefly at first so as to test out whether God has given them the ministry of the word. Give them opportunity, but not too much. Do not seal any gift and likewise do not spoil any meeting. If some are gifted, encourage them to speak longer next time. Some may have to be asked to speak more briefly later on. Constrain the gifted to proceed further; restrain the less gifted to cut the time shorter. Thus shall the meeting gather strength, and none of the mouths of the brothers will be sealed.

In serving the Lord, we must not only help people in every local assembly to know the Lord but also to discover new gifts. How can we find these gifts? It is in the meeting for the exercise of gifts. During such a meeting, we should have our eyes wide open. Encourage those on whom the Lord has laid His hand. Some like to speak, yet have neither the gift nor the ministry of the word. It is not necessary to forbid them to speak; simply ask them to speak less. Thus shall the young believers be helped as well as be given a chance to help others.

Ministry Meetings

This is the least important of all meetings; still it is a

part of God's established order and thus should not be neglected. Through such meetings, we may receive the supply of God's word. We may have the opportunity to hear the word when an apostle comes our way or when some teachers and prophets reside with us. I do not suggest this is not an important meeting; I merely say it is the simplest. Nevertheless, there are also matters to be learned in this meeting. When people come, they should learn to be punctual, lest they compel others to wait. They should follow the directions of the ushers and not insist on choosing their own seats. They should also bring their own Bibles and hymnbooks.

1. LET HEARTS BE OPEN

In attending such meetings, on the spiritual side the first preparation is that the heart must be open. He who listens with prejudice will never get anything. He whose heart is closed will not receive any blessing from God. Let no one sit there to criticize. It is the hearer, not the critic, whom God will bless. I often say that whether a message is well delivered or not depends half on the preacher and half on the audience. No preacher can carry a meeting if he is met with closed hearts, tightly shut minds, or critical attitudes.

2. LET SPIRITS BE OPEN

As the heart needs to be open, so must the spirit. It is of great importance that the spirit of the audience be open. When a true minister of the word is ministering, his spirit is open. If he can touch an open spirit in the audience, then his spirit will be strengthened. If he does not meet a responsive spirit in the meeting or if he encounters an indifferent or closed spirit, his own spirit will turn back as the dove returned to the ark. The spirit of both the preacher and the audience must be released. The greater the release of the spirit of the audience, the stronger the spirit of the prophet becomes. If the spirit of the brothers and sisters does not come forth, neither can that of the prophet. Whether the word is released depends in large measure on the hearers. Therefore, learn to be tender and meek. Let us open our spirits that the Holy Spirit may come forth! Let us not be full of coldness, death, or opinions. Let us contribute to the spirit of the meeting, not obstruct it. Our spirits can either help or hinder the release of the spirit of the prophet. If new believers learn the lesson here, they will contribute to the strength of the meeting.

The above are the five different types of meetings which we find in the Bible. I believe Christianity has in its very nature the need to assemble. If we know how to meet, then the next generation will become stronger. May we gird ourselves that we may arrive at the goal which God has set for us. May God be gracious to us.

THE LORD'S DAY

I was in the Spirit on the Lord's day, and I heard behind me a great voice, as of a trumpet . . .

Rev. 1:10

This is the day which Jehovah hath made; We will rejoice and be glad in it.

Ps. 118:24

And upon the first day of the week, when we were gathered together to break bread, Paul discoursed with them, intending to depart on the morrow; and prolonged his speech until midnight.

Acts 20:7

Upon the first day of the week let each one of you lay by him in store, as he may prosper, that no collections be made when I come.

1 Cor. 16:2

God's Creation and Rest

God measured each day by the evening and the morning. He repaired the earth in six days, and on the seventh day He rested. About two thousand five hundred years later, He gave the ten commandments in which He charged men to remember the Sabbath. All the other commandments are "shall" and "shall not"; only the fourth commandment calls us to remember God's work. In other words, this remembrance points back to the creation of the world. It is to recall how God restored the world in six days and how He then rested on the seventh day. Therefore, the seventh day is God's Sabbath. After more than two thousand years from the creation, God gave His Sabbath to men with the charge that they should rest on that day.

When God first gave the seventh day, the Sabbath, to men, He desired them to rest physically. Since God Himself rested on the seventh day and ceased from all His labor, He also desired men to work for six days and rest on the seventh day. The Sabbath was originally God's day of rest but He gave it to men, especially to the people of Israel in order that they too might cease from all works and thus might rest. The thought of rest on the Sabbath is quite clear in the Old Testament.

Man's First Day—The Original Seventh Day

The things in the Old Testament are but shadows of things in the New Testament. The Sabbath which God gave to men, like all other Old Testament types, has also a spiritual significance. God's seventh day was actually man's first day. God had just created man on the sixth day. So it became man's first day of life on the earth. Furthermore, as soon as he was created, he entered into God's rest. God worked for six days and then rested on the seventh day. But man first rested for one day before he started to work for six days. This is quite obvious.

The fulfillment of the meaning of the Sabbath comes by entering into God's rest. But to enter into God's rest, we must accept His work. God works, so we work; God rests, so we rest. We do not enter into God's rest on our seventh day, for we never worked six days before resting. As a matter of fact, we rest before we work. This is a very basic principle to us, a principle basic to the gospel. Rest before work, rest preceding work—this is the gospel. God shows that in first providing us rest, He also enables us to work afterward. Praise God, having rested we are able to work.

For this reason, it was a great sin for anyone to violate the Sabbath. God gave this day for people to rest. How could men consider it as nothing if they worked on that day? Violation of the Sabbath was as sinful as Moses' striking the rock with the rod (see Num. 20). God commanded Moses to speak to the rock that it might give forth water; He did not charge him to strike the rock with the rod. This was because the rock had been struck once and so should not be smitten again. Moses needed only to give a command and the rock would flow forth with living water. When he struck it the second time, he destroyed the work of God. As a consequence, Moses never entered the land of Canaan. On the same principle, how can anyone say that it does not matter if he violates the Sabbath? Judging from God's truth, it matters a great deal. Man ought to enjoy God's rest before he ventures to work. He needs to have entered into the value of the gospel before he starts to work. First, he enters God's rest; then he can do God's work. If he violates the Sabbath, he destroys what it typifies. Hence, the Sabbath has a very prominent place in the Old Testament.

During the Old Testament days, if anyone went out to

the field on the Sabbath and gathered sticks for burning, he was to be stoned to death. This was because he had violated the Sabbath. By his actions he seemed to claim that he was capable of working and conducting himself well without having to enter first into God's rest. God rested on the Sabbath because He was satisfied with His work. If we are satisfied with God's work, we too should rest on the Sabbath as an expression of our acceptance of His work. For this reason, God commanded at the very outset that "the seventh day is a sabbath unto Jehovah thy God: in it thou shalt not do any work, thou, nor thy son, nor thy daughter, thy man-servant, nor thy maid-servant, nor thy cattle, nor thy stranger that is within thy gates" (Ex. 20:10). Everyone in the house must cease working. This is the picture given us in the Old Testament.

The Sabbath in the New Testament

When it came to New Testament days, conditions were somewhat changed. It seems as if the Sabbath day became more positive in the New Testament. Whereas in the Old Testament there was the emphasis on not doing any work, in the New Testament the Lord Jesus read the law and the prophets in the synagogue on the Sabbath. That which was originally intended for physical rest had by then become a day for spiritual pursuit. This element is not found in the Old Testament. So there is progression in the New Testament: to physical rest has been added the hearing of the law and the prophets. The principle of setting apart one day out of seven for God is implied.

It is indeed marvelous to see the Sabbath in the New Testament turned into something more positive. On the

Sabbath, people attended the synagogue to listen to the law and to the prophets. The Lord Jesus preached in the synagogue on the Sabbath; the apostles, including Paul himself, also preached and reasoned in the synagogue on the Sabbath. The Sabbath became not only a day of rest but also a day of positive use. Special emphasis was now laid on the spiritual side.

The Change of Position of the Sabbath

In studying the Bible, we must pay attention to the spirit of the Word. If we have a teachable spirit, we will notice how frequently there are shifts of position in the Bible. This is what we mean by finding facts. For in these facts, light is hidden. When the facts change, light also changes. Such, we find, is the case with the Sabbath. In the very beginning, the seventh day was the Sabbath. If anyone did not rest, he was punished by being stoned to death.

The four gospels show us that the Lord Jesus was raised on the first day of the week. He manifested Himself afterward five different times on that same first day of the week. The book of Acts records that the day of Pentecost also fell on the first day of the week since the fiftieth day was actually the first day of another week. The first day of the week is the eighth day. Nowhere in the Bible are we told that God ordered the Lord's day to be substituted for the Sabbath. No, God simply made the change seen in the facts.

In reading the Old Testament, it seems as if each seven days forms a period which ends with the seventh day. According to typology, the first seven days speak of the old creation. God worked for six days and then He rested on the seventh day. This is the story of the old creation, concluded with the seventh day. God did not divide the days into months and years only; He especially divided them into weeks.

If the resurrection of the Lord Jesus had taken place at the end of the week, then the Old and the New Testaments would have been confused forever, for we then would have had the new creation and the old creation in the same week. But the Lord Jesus rose on the first day of the week, thereby marking a new beginning—that of the new creation. We desire that new believers would remember this principle in the Bible, that one day out of each seven days is set apart for spiritual purposes. On that day, no secular work should be done so that one may devote the time to spiritual affairs. The church in the New Testament has been quite naturally led by the Holy Spirit into having this day on the first day of the week, the resurrection day of the Lord Jesus. Unlike those living in Old Testament days, we are not charged as to what we cannot do. No, in the New Covenant there is no Sabbath, only the Lord's day. God does not forbid the doing of certain things on the Lord's day as He formerly had done for the Sabbath.

The Sabbath in the Old Testament is but a type. With the coming of the reality, the type has passed away. The Sabbath, like the sacrifice of bullocks and sheep, has passed away. The gospel has come. Man has entered into rest through the gospel. He is now able to serve God. This is the reality of the Sabbath.

So, under the New Covenant we have nothing to do with the Sabbath. This is not as simple as it may seem. If our interpretation of Revelation chapters 2 and 3 is correct, the legalistic party found in Christianity will be on the increase. New believers, therefore, must know the difference being presented here.

The principle of the Sabbath is as much a part of the gospel as our Lord's sacrifice on the cross. All the Old Testament cattle and sheep point to the Lamb of God, the Lord Jesus. When He came, the cattle and sheep were no longer effectual. Should anyone today offer a bullock or a sheep as a sacrifice, he blasphemes our Lord. The Lord has become the sacrifice, so how can a bullock or sheep be offered again? In the same manner, now that the gospel has come, people can rest in God. God has finished all the work of redemption in the cross of His Son. We who listen to God's Word enter into rest, not into work. Through the gospel we are enabled to rest before God. Only after entering into this rest can we rise up to serve. Since the rest of the gospel has come, naturally the Sabbath day has passed away. For us believers, the Sabbath has passed away just as much as has the sacrifice of cattle and sheep. Just as there are now no more cattle and sheep to be offered, so there is no longer a Sabbath day.

Let us be very careful in the use of the Word. Nowhere in the Bible can we find a *Christian* Sabbath day, for these two are contradictory. If we are Christians, then there is no Sabbath. If there is a Sabbath, then we are not Christians. The Sabbath belongs to the Old Testament. In the New Testament it has passed away.

The Lord's Day in the New Testament

The New Covenant, however, does have its own day, based not on the Sabbath, but on one day out of every seven days. The Sabbath day has not been changed to become the Lord's day; another day entirely has been chosen. Under the Old Covenant God chose the seventh day, but in the New Covenant He chose the first day of the week.

The fourth commandment says, "Remember the sabbath day, to keep it holy . . . but the seventh day is a sabbath unto Jehovah thy God: in it thou shalt not do any work . . ." (Ex. 20:8, 10a). But under the New Covenant, when God selected another day, He did not prohibit anything. Nothing negative was ever mentioned. He never stated what may not be done on the Lord's day; He only told us what should and can be done. The prime characteristic of the Lord's day lies in its positiveness.

There is a very clear distinction between the Old and the New Covenants. So far as God's appointed days are concerned, one came at the end of the week while the other came at the beginning of the week. The Old Covenant terminated with the seventh day; the New Covenant commenced with the first day of the week. The first week belonged exclusively to the old creation, but beginning on the first day of the next week there was only the new creation. There is absolutely no confusion, no mixing of the old and new within the same week. The Lord Jesus rose on the first day of the week; the church was born on the day of Pentecost, also the first day of the week.

Consequently, should anyone desire to go back and keep the seventh day, he confuses the New and the Old Covenants. There is absolutely no basis in the Bible for doing so. In reading Scripture, is it not surprising to find that seven days after the resurrection of the Lord, the disciples were found assembled together again on the first day of the second week? We do not know why they did not meet on the Sabbath day, but we do know that they did meet on the first day of the second week.

Scriptural Basis for the Lord's Day

We think the following passages are of great importance: "The stone which the builders rejected is become the head of the corner. This is Jehovah's doing; it is marvellous in our eyes. This is the day which Jehovah hath made; we will rejoice and be glad in it" (Ps. 118:22–24).

"Be it known unto you all, and to all the people of Israel, that in the name of Jesus Christ of Nazareth, whom ye crucified, whom God raised from the dead, even in him doth this man stand here before you whole. He is the stone which was set at nought of you the builders, which was made the head of the corner" (Acts 4:10–11).

Here the phrase is found "the stone rejected by the builders." Who decides whether a stone is usable or not? It is the builders. If the mason says that a certain stone is unfit to build the house, you do not need to ask anybody else. Whatever the builder decides is final. But a strange thing happened. The stone which the builders rejected became the head of the corner. God put upon it the most important responsibility. What the builders considered useless, God made the chief cornerstone. This is the Lord's doing. It is marvelous in our eyes. It is indeed marvelous. Verse 24, however, gives us an added marvel related to the Lord's day. "This is the day which Jehovah hath made; we will rejoice and be glad in it." The day which the Lord has appointed is the day when the stone rejected by the builders became the chief cornerstone.

It is a day when we will rejoice and be glad. All should fear God and rejoice in His presence. Let us, then, find out what day it was when the stone rejected by the builders became the head of the corner. This we discover in Acts 4:10–11. Verse 10 says, "Whom ye crucified, whom God raised from the dead." Verse 11 continues, "He is the stone which was set at nought of you the builders, which was made the head of the corner." In other words, this is the day of the resurrection of the Lord Jesus. God, not man, determined the day when He who was rejected by men was to be raised from the dead. Let there be no confusion. The Bible puts it very clearly that this is the day the Lord has made. What day is it? It is the day of resurrection. So let all the children of God gather in the name of God's Son on that day and be glad.

Do you see the difference between the Lord's day in the New Testament and the Sabbath day in the Old Testament? The latter is negative, full of "shalt not's" and the threat of the punishment of death; the former, though, is a day of great rejoicing.

Things to Be Done on the Lord's Day

In regard to the first day of the week, three things receive special attention in the Bible:

1. REJOICE—THE PROPER ATTITUDE

The first thing concerns our attitude. As we have just read, all the children of God should rejoice and be glad on the first day of the week, for this is the day our Lord was raised from the dead. There was no need to tell Peter and the other apostles to rejoice. During the days when their

Lord was laid in the tomb, they experienced great disappointment and sadness. Then they found that the tomb was empty! They could not but rejoice and be glad.

This is the day the Lord has made. Let us maintain an attitude of rejoicing. There is no other day as marvelous as this day, for this is the day of the resurrection of our Lord. On the first day of the week, the Lord came to gather with the apostles; He came again on the first day of the second week. He must have appeared to them at least five times on the first day of the week. Later on, the Holy Spirit came upon the apostles and those gathered together on the first day of the week. It was at that time that Peter's eyes were opened to see how the stone rejected by the builders had become the head of the corner as prophesied in Psalm 118. In His crucifixion He was rejected by the builders but by His resurrection He became the head of the corner. The Holy Spirit gave Peter this understanding. Who but the Holy Spirit could point out the Lord Jesus in this psalm? He was rejected by the builders, but in His resurrection, He became the head of the corner. This is the day the Lord has made; let us rejoice and be glad. It is the natural consequence of such a day.

2. ASSEMBLE TO BREAK BREAD

"And upon the first day of the week, when we were gathered together to break bread" (Acts 20:7a). Notice the grammatical structure here. The second clause is in apposition to the preceding phrase, meaning that the first day of the week is the time when they gathered to break bread. It does not point to any specific first day of the week, but simply refers to every first day of the week. So naturally this has become the day when all the churches gather to break bread in remembrance of the Lord. What day is more excellent than this, the first day of the week?

We today are people of the New Covenant. One of its characteristics is that we meet the Lord on the first day of the week. This is the day of His resurrection, a day in which we rejoice and are glad. We break bread to testify that our Lord has already died for us; we break bread to attest to the oneness of the church. Other than this one thing that we must do, there also are other things that can be done on this day.

The breaking of bread has two meanings in Scripture: one is to remember the Lord and the other is to fellowship with all the children of God. One shows our communion with God and His Christ; the other discloses our fellowship with the body of Christ which is the church. When we break the bread, we commune with our Lord, for the bread represents the Lord. But also when we break the bread, we fellowship with all the saints, because this same bread represents the church—we, being many, are one bread. For this reason, the Lord's day is the best time for us to fellowship with all of God's children as well as to commune with the Lord.

It is literally impossible for me to give the right hand of fellowship to every one of God's children on earth. Yet on each Lord's day, all the children of God touch the one bread. Wherever they may be, they touch the same bread as I. In this way I touch all the children of God. Here I meet all my brothers and sisters as well as my Lord. I not only have fellowship with those who break the bread with me in the meeting but also with all whose hands touch the bread throughout the world. We, being many, are one bread. As I break bread with them, I also fellowship with them.

New believers should learn to maintain an unclouded relationship with all God's children. They ought to learn love and forgiveness from the very outset. Who is it that the Bible teaches should not touch the Lord's table? It is he who is unforgiving. If he does not forgive, he is unfit to touch the bread. By not forgiving another's fault, he will have something between him and that other child of God We must neither be jealous of anyone nor refuse to fellowship with anyone. Nothing should be allowed to come between the brethren. Other than those who have been excommunicated for reasons of conduct or truth, we must not refuse fellowship to anybody. All God's children everywhere should be in fellowship. Hence, there is a very real need for forgiveness and love. May our hearts go out toward all of God's children.

"And upon the first day of the week, when we were gathered together to break bread"—this is the way distinctly laid before us in the Bible. It has nothing to do with the Sabbath. The one and only similarity is that both were chosen out of the week for a specific purpose. The Bible never sanctions any attempt to change the Sabbath into the Lord's day. Under the New Covenant God chose another day for us to remember our Lord.

3. GIVE

"Now concerning the collection for the saints, as I gave order to the churches of Galatia, so also do ye. Upon the first day of the week let each one of you lay by him in store, as he may prosper, that no collections be made when

I come" (1 Cor. 16:1–2). Here we find the second thing which should be done on the first day of the week. Paul repeated an order to the churches in Achaia that he formerly had given to the churches in Galatia. On each Lord's day there was something to be done. It is quite evident that during the apostolic time, the first day of the week was a special day.

If Paul wanted to find the Jews, he looked for them on the Sabbath; but if he wanted to find the Christians, he had to do it on the first day of the week. This was not only true of the churches in Achaia and in Galatia but also true of the churches everywhere, for the first day of the week is a very special day to Christians. On that day we break bread to remember the Lord. On that day we give as the Lord has prospered us. Is it not surprising to find that giving is to be done once a week, not once a month? Many wait until the end of the month and some even wait until the end of the year; but Paul tells us, we must balance our accounts before God on the first day of each week. We should lay aside our contribution to the Lord as He has prospered us each week.

I work throughout the week, so then I put aside a certain amount out of that with which the Lord has prospered me during that week and give it to Him. I always feel this is an excellent thing. We break bread on the one hand and give on the other hand. We remember how the Lord has given Himself to us; now we also give something to the Lord.

Remember that he who receives more from God ought to give more. Among all the praises and thanks to the Lord, giving is also reckoned as a sacrifice of praise (see Heb. 13:16). It is a sacrifice which we must offer. At the breaking of bread, we remember what the Lord has done for us. After the bread is broken, we lay before the Lord a token of that with which He has prospered us. We merely put into the Lord's hand that which He has first given us. To me, this is most beautiful. It is indeed an excellent thing to give on the Lord's day.

If you will pardon me, I would like to speak very frankly to new believers. According to the New Testament, there are only two things which we must definitely do. The Lord has not said, "What if a lamb falls into a pit?" or "What if there is a paralytic?" There is not the slightest hint of the old Sabbath, for it has already passed away. It has been fulfilled so far as its spiritual significance is concerned. We have arrived at its reality in the gospel. The type gives way to the antitype. The Old Testament dispensation is over. In the church, the Lord has chosen another day. On the Lord's day, the church should break bread and give offerings.

My brothers and sisters, do not come to meetings and give thoughtlessly. This is entirely wrong. You must carefully consider it before the Lord and have your offering ready as you come. Your coming to remember the Lord is not accidental; likewise, your giving should be planned and prearranged. On each Lord's day, set aside a portion of what the Lord has prospered you with and bring it to the Lord. Let each one decide his own percentage. Give more if you are given more; less if you have less. The important thing is that you give your portion joyfully.

It looks ugly for anyone to fish out some money from his pocket and cast it carelessly into the offering box. It is almost unbearable to see such an action. Before you come to the meeting, you should have your offering ready. An offering is as serious as the breaking of bread. The breaking of bread signifies what God has given me, while the offering represents that which I present to God as a sacrifice. Do remember that an offering is a sacrifice. I must prepare my heart, set aside a portion, and bring it to God.

I often think (I wonder if you have thought of this too?) how at His return the Lord will settle accounts with His servants—the servant with the one talent, the one with the two talents, and the one with the five talents. Each Lord's day is the time when we settle our accounts with the Lord, but one day the Lord will come and make a reckoning with us. He will examine how we have used the money and how much we have earned. Now, though, on the first day of each week, we make a reckoning with the Lord, saying, "Oh, Lord, I take out a portion of what I have earned during this week and offer it to you." If we do this every week, we will have no fear at the judgment seat. Nothing unexpected will happen to us for our accounts will have been in order week after week.

The first day of the week is different from the Sabbath of the Old Testament. It is not a day of judgment, nor is it merely a day for physical rest. The cessation of all work is not required. Neither is judgment pronounced on those who do work. This day rather points out what two things we especially ought to do: one is to come to the Lord in order to receive grace, and the other is to offer our gift to the Lord. It is a day for us to rejoice and be glad. It is the Lord's day.

We hope that new believers will enjoy the Lord's grace and serve Him well on His day. God has chosen this day of the week for us. The Bible calls it the Lord's day (see Rev.

1:10). Do not confuse the Lord's day with the day of the Lord.

In reading the writings of the so-called church fathers, we find many of them verify that the Lord's day points to the first day of the week. Many writings of the second and the third centuries attest to this fact. The day which the church gathered together during the second and the third centuries was the first day of the week, not the Sabbath. It is not true to say that the day was originally on the Sabbath but was changed to the first day of the week during the fourth century. At least twenty to thirty church fathers, starting with the disciples of the apostle John and continuing through the second, third, and fourth centuries, all agree that it was the first day of the week.

The Lord's Day—the First Day of the Week

Why do we deal with this subject? What is the practical value of it? The application involved is most significant. The Lord has set apart one day in the week and called it the Lord's day. If you ask me whether you can travel or buy things on this day, I frankly acknowledge that I do not know. But one thing I do know, and that is, this day is the Lord's day, a day which belongs to Him. So you can do on this day whatever the Lord does and you cannot do what He does not do.

Throughout my life, I should set aside the Lord's day as a very special day. If I live till seventy years of age (see Ps. 90:10), I can bow my head and say that out of these seventy years, I have taken ten years wholly for the Lord. It is very exact indeed. I set aside the first day of each week for the Lord. The day is not mine, but the Lord's. Its hours do not belong to me, but to the Lord. If I rest, I rest for the Lord; if I work, I work for the Lord. Whether I do a thing or do not do a thing, it is all unto the Lord. There is no flavor of the Sabbath, no hint of punishment in it. I just simply offer the day completely to the Lord.

I think the apostle John spoke well when he wrote, "I was in the Spirit on the Lord's day" (Rev. 1:10). As he waited upon the Lord, he came into the Spirit. Many can testify that they are moved by the Holy Spirit on the Lord's day. May this day be the day when the Holy Spirit moves the church. May this be a day of blessing to us. It is well to say, "I am in the Spirit on the Lord's day." I hope all new believers will see what the Lord's day is and thus offer it to Him saying, "Lord, this is your day." It will be a great blessing to the church if many will begin from their youth to offer this day to the Lord. "O Lord, on this day I joyfully break the bread in remembrance of You; I also bring what I have and offer it to You. All my time throughout this day is to be spent for You." If this is true, the blessing of God will be poured down abundantly upon the church.

HYMN SINGING

Understanding Hymn Singing

We would like now to consider the matter of hymn singing. We need to instruct new believers how to sing hymns. Even as prayer is often neglected, perhaps even more so is singing.

1. KNOW THE HYMNS

We wish to point out that our intention is not to make musicians out of the brothers and sisters. That would be purely worldly. What we do desire, though, is that they may know the hymns they sing. This we consider to be of great importance. In a meeting, those who sing the loudest all too frequently are those whose hearts are least touched. Our aim is not to produce fine voices or good music. What we want to appreciate before God is the hymn itself.

2. CULTIVATE A DELICATE FEELING

In the Bible we find that as well as prophecies, history, doctrines, and commandments, there are also hymns. One basic reason for the presence of these hymns in Scripture, I believe, is to train God's people to have finer, more delicate feelings.

Let me enlarge upon this point. So far as human sentiment is concerned, we have both delicate and rough feelings. When a person is angry, he manifests a crude feeling. When one is insensitive, the emotions he shows are neither gentle nor polite. God wants us to love, to show kindness, to be merciful and gracious. He wishes us to be sympathetic. His will is that we sing while in prison, that we praise His name in time of suffering. All these require delicate feelings. When one loves, his feeling is most exquisite. When he is merciful, his sensation is indeed soft and tender. When he forgives, his emotion is of the choicest kind. How very different is a crude feeling from a forgiving spirit. How tender and delicate is our Lord's sentiment when He shows mercy to us.

The way God leads His children is toward having their senses exercised more and more in tenderness and delicacy. He does not want us to become increasingly rough. The world in training its soldiers teaches them to be more insensitive. A man's emotion's have to be developed in that direction if he is to fight and kill. But the Christian direction is totally the opposite. God guides our feeling toward greater tenderness and delicacy.

3. Man's Tenderest Feelings Expressed

Poems or hymns show man's tenderest feelings. The sentiment we exhibit in prayer cannot exceed in its delicateness that expressed in singing hymns. God purposes that we should have delicate feelings. For this reason, He gives us all kinds of poems in abundance in the Bible. We not only have the Psalms, the Song of Songs, and Lamentations but also other poems mingled in the historical sections and the commandments. Even in Paul's letters, so full of doctrine, he has unconsciously interspersed some poems.

One thing marvelous to observe is that the longer a person is a Christian and the more he has learned before God, the more tender his feelings become. On the contrary, if he has had few dealings with God and has learned but little, he seems to be rough and unpoetic.

Suppose you come to the meeting today wearing a pair of heavy, sturdy shoes; your steps can be heard from quite a distance. You look more like a soldier than a Christian. If you bump into this chair and that table as you walk in, you do not give the impression of being a singer. For brothers and sisters to be able to sing hymns, they themselves must be fine, like a poem. From the day you are saved, God starts to cultivate delicate feelings within you. Your former crude sensations will not help you to be a Christian. To be a good Christian, you must have delicate feelings.

4. Incense to God

I have used this metaphor before. Incense in Scripture sometimes represents prayer and sometimes a poem of praise unto God. Incense comes from trees. It is the sap or juice of the tree—an extraction of the very life of the tree. Made into incense and burned before God, it gives forth a most delicate savor. It is not the burning of wood or bark or leaves, but the consuming of the exuded juice and sap. It is something which flows from within and thus becomes a poem of praise to God.

Three Basic Requirements of Hymns

What is a hymn or a poem? According to what we read in the Bible, a proper hymn or poem must fulfill at least three basic requirements. The lack of any of these three requirements renders the hymn unusable.

1. SOUNDNESS OF TRUTH

The first criterion for a hymn to be usable is soundness in truth. Many hymns are well qualified in other areas, but if there are errors in truth they lead God's children into a wrong sentiment. It is extremely difficult for people to approach God while they are filled with human errors. In singing, we must let our delicate feeling ascend to God. If there is error in truth, we deceive ourselves and thus fail to touch reality. God never allows us to deal with Him according to the hymns we sing. He permits us to deal with Him only in accordance to the truth we hold. In other words, we can approach God only in truth. Things that are not of the truth are not acceptable.

EXAMPLE 1
CONSCIENCE MISTAKEN FOR HEART

I have read gospel hymns with words such as, "the blood of Jesus washes our hearts." After having gone over the New Testament more than a hundred times, I have never met such a scriptural text that states that the blood of Jesus washes our hearts. The nearest to it is found in the book of Hebrews which says, "Having our hearts sprinkled from an evil conscience" (Heb. 10:22b). The blood does not cleanse the heart; it cleanses the conscience. Having our sins washed by the blood of our Lord, our conscience no longer accuses us before God. Do you see how a little error can make us practice an untruth? Our delicate sentiment is misapplied. This is a very serious matter. God's children will be led into a wrong position if the hymn they sing is erroneous in truth.

Our hearts are not cleansed by the blood. As a matter of fact, our hearts can never be washed clean. The heart of man is deceitful above all things; it cannot be cleansed by washing. The Bible teaching on the matter of the heart is, "a new heart also will I give you . . . and I will take away the stony heart out of your flesh, and I will give you a heart of flesh" (Ez. 36:26). When one believes on the Lord, rather than wash his old heart, God gives him a new heart. So the truth is that our conscience, not our heart, is cleansed of its offense. Truth demands absolute accuracy.

EXAMPLE 2

LACK OF DISPENSATIONAL CLARITY

Many hymns are rather vague as to whom the words refer or what time is meant. Whether the words are to be sung as coming from Abraham or Moses, Peter or us, Jews or Christians, we do not know. We are not sure if they are to be sung under the Old Covenant or under the New Covenant. They lack dispensational clarity. In singing them, sometimes you feel as if you are singing the songs of the angels who have no personal experience of redemption. At other times, you feel as if you are still under the Old Covenant, for there is no confidence or assurance in the songs. These hymns do not delineate a clear understanding of God's dispensational dealings. They fail to show us that we are now in the dispensation of grace. They lead us to a wrong standing. I know of one or two hymns which should only be sung by those who have not sinned and who have no need of the blood. Because of this type of error, we need to notice the accuracy of dispensational truth without which no hymn can be reckoned usable.

EXAMPLE 3

LACK OF CHRISTIAN CONFIDENCE

Many hymns are written without Christian assurance. This makes singing them very difficult. They express the hope, the longing, the search for salvation, but there is nothing of the confidence that a Christian should normally possess. Let us remember: when we draw nigh to God, we come full of faith and confidence. If the singing gives one the feeling of being in the outer court, then the singer is not a child of God but only a person who would like to be inside. This creates an almost insurmountable problem, for it immediately puts the Christian in a false position. A Christian position is one full of confidence, knowing that he is saved. All hymns which lack assurance should not be sung by Christians because they are not consistent with the truth.

EXAMPLE 4

MISCONCEPTION OF ENTERING INTO GLORY

AFTER DEATH

Another common fault in hymns is the wrong concept of a Christian's entering into glory right after death. Many hymns give such an impression. We know, however, that man does not enter into glory after death. Entry into glory is quite a different matter. After death we wait for resurrection. The Lord entered into glory after resurrection and so shall we. This is the clear teaching of the Bible. Hymns which induce the sentiment of glory after death ought not to be sung for they are contrary to fact.

2. POETIC FORM AND STRUCTURE

All good hymns must possess a poetic form and structure. A hymn is supposed to be poetical. If the truth is accurate but the form not poetic, it cannot be considered a good hymn. Soundness in truth alone does not make a hymn. There needs to be poetic form and structure.

A hymn should not be in the form of a sermon. How can we sing a sermon? I remember once I argued with a brother over a hymn, the first line of which was, "The true God created heaven, earth, and men." This could be good for preaching, but it would be difficult to sing. If this hymn were given to David to sing, I am sure he would rather fight Goliath than sing it! As a matter of fact, it sounds more like fighting Goliath. Its sentiment is quite crude. It is doctrinal but not poetical.

Not any of the Psalms in the Bible are crude; all are exquisitely delicate. Each one is written in poetic form and structure. God's thought is expressed in poetic words.

In writing a hymn, it is not the meter alone that counts. The whole song must be poetically constructed.

3. TOUCHES REALITY

A hymn requires sound truth, poetic form and structure, and also a spiritual touch.

WITH SPIRITUAL SENTIMENT

To illustrate, let us use Psalm 51 which tells of David's repentance. The truth is right and the psalm is poetically constructed. Its words are intricately designed; they are not ejaculatory cries. In reading this psalm, you are aware of David's repentance; yet you would never just treat it as doctrine, for it touches spiritual reality. Hence it draws from you a spiritual feeling. This we call the burden of the psalm. David repents, and this deep sense of repentance pervades the whole psalm.

In other words, a hymn must be able to touch your emotions deeply. It can either make you cry or rejoice as the content dictates. It should not be just poetically constructed and yet void of the power to move people to cry or to rejoice. A poetic sentiment is necessary to a hymn, a feeling which one cannot fail to sense. How can you sing a hymn on repentance and feel like laughing or sing a hymn of praise and not feel uplifted?

DEPENDABLE IN FEELING

One basic demand for a hymn is that it must induce a real feeling; that is, a feeling which touches spiritual reality. It ought not to be a hymn on consecration and yet not incite a desire to consecrate; nor should it be a hymn of praise without stirring the heart to praise; nor ought it to be a hymn for brokenness before God while producing an adverse emotion of pride in oneself.

A hymn must not only be accurate in objective truth; it should also be effective upon the heart. Furthermore, if it is a good hymn, it should touch something of spiritual reality in your life. These three characteristics must coexist in a hymn: accuracy of truth, poetic construction, and the touch of spiritual reality. A hymn which merely presents subject matter does not qualify as a good hymn.

I often feel that the collection of the Psalms has a special feature, that is, its expression of the psalmist's true feelings.

When the psalmist is happy, he can leap for joy. When he is sad, he can cry. His feelings are genuine. He does not mince words, but expresses his real feelings. Believers should be told that a hymn needs to be accurate in doctrine, in form, and in feeling.

Three Different Types of Hymns

There are three different types of hymns in the Bible.

1. HYMNS TOWARD GOD

The principle objective of a hymn is for it to be sung to God. Hence, most of the Psalms in the Old Testament are of this nature. In fact, most hymns should be Godward.

2. HYMNS TOWARD MEN

Proverbs is also poetic writing, but it is of a different type, for it is directed to men. Among Christians, however, such hymns should be limited in number. The vast majority of the Psalms are Godward, though there are some which are manward. In recent decades, so-called sacred songs have become extremely popular. From the time of Sankey on, sacred songs have been gradually welcomed by the churches. Nonetheless, these sacred songs should not occupy too prominent a place in the church since their direction is toward men. If there are too many hymns of this type, they will destroy the right proportion set forth in the Bible. Generally speaking, hymns should be Godward; hymns that are manward are permissible only in a small number. Too many of the latter are contrary to the significance of hymns. Hymns of praise, of thanksgiving, and of prayer are all directed toward God. Gospel hymns and

95

hymns for exhortation are of the second type and these are directed toward men.

3. HYMNS TOWARD SELF

In the Bible, especially in the book of the Psalms, we find a third type of hymn—those sung neither to God nor to men but to self. In many places there are expressions such as, "O my soul!" It is the communion of myself with my soul before God, the fellowship of myself with my heart, the consultation or communication between my heart and myself. All who know God and who have communed with God will understand this matter of communion with their own heart. So in this third type of hymn, I commune with myself and I consult with my heart. I sing unto myself, calling myself and awakening myself; I make decisions, I remind myself. Usually at the end of these hymns one is led to God, for a spiritual person cannot be in communion with himself long without being drawn to God. His fellowship with his heart invariably changes into communion with God.

ILLUSTRATIONS FROM THE PSALMS

Let us illustrate these three types of hymns from the collection of the Psalms.

PSALMS TOWARD GOD

Psalm 51 definitely turns Godward. This is a well-known psalm, one which depicts David's repentance after his having sinned. Repentance is always toward God. "Have mercy upon me, O God, according to thy lovingkindness." It begins with God. If we judge this psalm by the three basic requirements of a hymn, we must concede that this psalm is accurate in truth, poetic in expression, and spiritual in sentiment. I like to touch the heartbeat of the psalmist. "And in the hidden part thou wilt make me to know wisdom. Purify me with hyssop, and I shall be clean: Wash me, and I shall be whiter than snow" (vv. 6b-7). Both the diction and the inward feeling are exquisitely poetic. These are not simple statements; rather they are poetic expressions, full of emotion.

PSALMS TOWARD MEN

Not a few of the Psalms are directed toward men. For example, take Psalm 37. There are many passages here which are intended for men. They sound like preaching— preaching in poetry.

Both Psalms 1 and 2 may be considered as preaching to men, but they also both turn to the Lord.

Psalm 133 speaks of the anointing oil poured upon men. "Behold, how good and how pleasant it is for brethren to dwell together in unity! It is like the precious oil upon the head, that ran down upon the beard, even Aaron's beard; that came down upon the skirt of his garments . . ." It sounds like a sermon, yet it is truly a poem.

PSALMS TOWARD SELF

The third type in the Psalms deals with fellowship with one's heart. The most distinctive one is Psalm 103 in which a man communes with his own heart before God. "Bless Jehovah, O my soul; and all that is within me, bless his holy name." This is a well-fitted couplet. The writer's feeling is reinforced by expressing the same thought in two different ways. In poems we often meet such reiteration. It helps to heighten the sentiment until it reaches its peak.

Also in Psalm 121 we find consultation within oneself. "I will lift up mine eyes unto the mountains: from whence shall my help come? My help cometh from Jehovah, who made heaven and earth." The psalmist himself both asks and answers the question. It is a communion and consultation of one's self with his heart before God.

ILLUSTRATIONS FROM HYMNALS

We should study carefully the hymns we sing. They should be selected according to the three requirements we have given. Some hymns are strong in the first and the third requirements, yet weak in the second requirement. For instance, the hymns written by A. B. Simpson are very accurate in sentiment and in truth, but sometimes our brother's hymns sound more like sermons. Such hymns are not poetic enough. I suppose that those who preach a lot ought to write less hymns!

Let us now look at some representative hymns.

HYMNS TOWARD GOD

These hymns need not always be addressed to God, nor must God's name be mentioned, so long as they are sung unto God.

EXAMPLE

> 1. Hark! ten thousand voices crying,
>   "Lamb of God!" with one accord;
>   Thousand thousand saints replying
>   Wake at once the echoing chord.

I think rarely in these twenty centuries has there been

any hymn which surpasses this one in grandeur. The hymn was written by J. N. Darby. When he first wrote it, it had fifteen stanzas; but in 1881 when he and Mr. Wigram changed it for singing, they shortened it to seven stanzas. Later on, several different ones tampered with it, a few bettering it somewhat while others worsened it.

In reading through the hymn, you naturally feel you are being brought into the scene of Revelation, chapters 4 and 5. It impresses you with the condition of the universe after the ascension of our Lord. In it, you see Calvary, resurrection, and ascension. The heaven is filled with glory; a name is given to the Lord Jesus. To this name, every knee bows in worship and every tongue confesses Him Lord. All over the heaven, the earth, and beneath the earth there arise songs of praise. The whole universe is singing His praises. How enthusiastic the atmosphere is! Everyone comes to praise His name. Such a hymn could never be written by anyone less spiritually competent.

The sound suddenly breaks forth—"Hark! ten thousand voices crying." The ten thousand voices together cry out. I, a little Christian, small as a worm, am included in the "Hark! ten thousand voices crying, Lamb of God! with one accord." Together we uplift the Lamb with one heart. Darby, when writing, seems to slip into the rank of the saints in the line of response, "Thousand thousand saints replying, wake at once the echoing chord." At this moment, everyone rejoins the anthem. It recalls Revelation 4 and 5 where the Lamb of God alone is uplifted as being worthy. On the one hand, there are ten thousand times ten thousand, and thousands upon thousands saying with a great voice, "Worthy is the Lamb that hath been slain to receive the power, and riches, and wisdom, and might, and honor, and glory, and blessing." Before their voices subside, "every created thing which is in the heaven, and on the earth, and under the earth, and on the sea, and all things that are in them," respond with, "Unto him that sitteth on the throne, and unto the Lamb, be the blessing and the honor, and the glory, and the dominion, for ever and ever." How does the response sound to human ears? "Wake at once the echoing chord." It comes like an explosion of unlimited force. At this moment, you sense that you are like a tiny little one being ushered into a scene of great magnificence. This hymn begins with a grandeur which makes it one of the great praises of the universe. Although God's name is not mentioned, it is evident that everything is directed toward Him.

> 2. "Praise the Lamb!"—the chorus waking,
>   All in heav'n together throng;
>   Loud and far, each tongue partaking,
>   Rolls around the endless song.

One stanza follows closely after another. "Praise the Lamb" comes from all sides. All in heaven throng together for the single purpose of singing praises. This leads us to the thought of Philippians 2 where every tongue confesses Jesus Christ is Lord. The confession is heard everywhere; it rolls around the whole universe.

> 3. Grateful incense this, ascending
>   Ever to the Father's throne;
>   Every knee to Jesus bending,
>   All the mind in heav'n is one.

From the voice (verse 1) to the tongue (verse 2), the hymn proceeds on to the grateful incense that ascends to the Father's throne (verse 3). Not only does every mouth shout, but also every heart rises as incense toward God. The Lamb of God is on every lip and the Father is on every heart. It seems to affirm that redemption and salvation are one, for they are indeed inseparable. The plan and the finished work are indivisible. The Father gives His only-begotten Son to us, and now our hearts go back to God. Praises break forth from grateful hearts and ascend as incense toward God.

Praise alone is not sufficient. From the mouth, we are led to the knee. All tongues shall praise, and all knees shall bow. How very poetic is the line which follows: "All the mind in heav'n is one." This is not preaching; it is the delicate feeling of one whose heart ascends toward the Father and whose tongue and knees respond to the Son. There is a sigh of relief expressed, noticing that all the minds of heaven are one. Indeed, the minds of heaven are one.

> 4. All the Father's counsels claiming
>   Equal honors to the Son,
>   All the Son's effulgence beaming,
>   Makes the Father's glory known.

Here you touch the Son as well as the Father. Glory is the substance within; effulgence is the manifestation without. What the Father has is glory, but when His glory is manifested in the Son it is effulgence. The Father's glory is the Son's effulgence; the Son's effulgence is the beaming of the Father's glory. To one who knows God, he understands this inward relationship between the Father and the Son.

Counsel springs from within, but it is used to claim equal honor to the Son. This is not the Father's work, but the Father's counsel, the Father's plan. What does the wisdom of the Father undertake to do? It undertakes to show the world that the Son has equal honor.

> 5. By the Spirit all pervading,
>   Hosts unnumbered round the Lamb,
>   Crowned with light and joy unfading,
>   Hail Him as the great "I AM."

He who has touched the Father and the Son will go on to touch the Spirit. "By the Spirit all pervading." When the Holy Spirit comes, He pervades the whole universe. He crowns all with light and joy and inspires them to hail the great "I AM." What is the source of their unfading joy? It is the great "I AM" whom they hail. We are thus brought into eternity, and eternity is brought to us. Let me tell you, this is indeed a song of praise, and a great one too.

> 6. Joyful now the wide creation
>   Rests in undisturbed repose,
>   Blest in Jesu's full salvation
>   Sorrow now nor thraldom knows.

It seems as if the writer pauses and looks around at the hosts that surround the Lamb. What is revealed on the faces of these singers? It is the joy of the new creation that rests in undisturbed repose. Everyone is blessed in the full salvation of the Lord. Sorrow and thraldom have become things of the past. All problems have been solved, and all are bathed in the joy and rest of His full salvation.

> 7. Hark! still louder swells the singing,
>   As the notes are heard again;
>   Through creation's vault is ringing
>   Joy's response, Amen! Amen!

I gaze and gaze upon this new creation. Hark! the voices of praise arise again. A most wonderful thing happens, "Joy's response, Amen! Amen!" From the whole universe is the voice of praise and from everywhere comes the response of amen.

HYMNS TOWARD MEN

Let us choose a verse and chorus from a hymn by A. B. Simpson and a hymn by A. J. Flint as representative of this type.

EXAMPLE 1

> "Hark! a voice from heav'n proclaiming,
>   "It is done."
> Faith repeats the echo claiming,
>   "It is done."
> Chorus:
>   Hear the message from the throne,
>   Claim the promise, doubting one;
>   God hath spoken, "It is done."
>   Faith has answer'd, "It is done."
>   Pray'r is over, praise begun.
>   Hallelujah, "It is done."
>   A. B. Simpson

"Hark! a voice from heav'n proclaiming, 'It is done.' " This is quite majestic. "Faith repeats the echo claiming, 'It is done!' " is rather ordinary. The first line of the chorus, "Hear the message from the throne," does not sound like poetry. But what follows is really good. "Claim the promise, doubting one." "Claim"—it is as if you come to God and claim something for yourself. How appropriate is this word. "God hath spoken, 'It is done.' Faith has answered,

'It is done.' " These are strong expressions. The next line is most accurate in truth, "Pray'r is over, praise begun." Naturally, the conclusion is "Hallelujah, 'It is done.' "

EXAMPLE 2

1. Though we may waver, He remaineth steadfast,
   And all His words are sure;
   From everlasting unto everlasting
   His promises endure.

2. Though we may wander, He will not forsake us,
   Truer than earthly friend;
   He never fails our trust, for having loved us,
   He loves unto the end.

3. Unto the end; we doubt Him, we deny Him,
   We wound Him, we forget;
   We get some earthly idol up between us
   Without one faint regret.

4. And when it falls or crumbles, and in anguish
   We seek this changeless Friend,
   Lo, He receives us, comforts and forgives us,
   And loves us to the end.

A. J. Flint

This hymn was written by Annie Johnson Flint and is directed toward men. It is quite poetic in composition. Its truth is accurate, and its sentiment is deep. The words she uses are very Christian; there is not even the slightest corruption of worldly expression.

The last stanza touches the peak: "And when it (the earthly idol) falls or crumbles." The idol we have set up has come to nothing. "And in anguish we seek this changeless Friend"—the Friend whom we had forgotten. "Lo, He receives us, comforts and forgives us, and loves us to the end." This reaches the highest realm for when the Lord brings us back to Himself, He does not even mention the past. It is as if nothing has ever happened. How poetic, how true, and how sensitive!

Notice also the two phrases, "unto the end" in stanzas two and three. First, "He never fails our trust, for having loved us, He loves us unto the end"; then, "Unto the end; we doubt Him, we deny Him, we wound Him, we forget." She repeats first how the Lord loves us, and turns afterward to our problem of being unfaithful to Him. Miss Flint was truly a poetess; both her feeling and her expression are poetic.

The point I want to stress is this: unless brothers and sisters learn how to read hymns, their feelings will not be delicate. That is why we should read all the Psalms in the Bible as well as the hymns we use with great care.

HYMNS TOWARD SELF

There are not many hymns which express communion with one's own heart. Some that are of this type are too rough in their feeling. They seem to lack in deep experience before God. They sound as if the author writes casually without having gone through deep trials and sufferings. The following hymn, however, is just the opposite; its feeling is very delicate.

EXAMPLE

1. If the path I travel
   Lead me to the cross;
   If the way Thou choosest
   Lead to pain and loss;

Let the compensation
Daily, hourly, be
Shadowless communion,
Blessed Lord, with Thee.

2. If there's less of earth joy,
Give, Lord, more of heaven.
Let the spirit praise Thee,
Though the heart be riven;
If sweet earthly ties, Lord,
Break at Thy decree,
Let the tie that binds us,
Closer, sweeter, be.

3. Lonely though the pathway,
Cheer it with Thy smile;
Be Thou my companion
Through earth's little while;
Selfless may I live, Lord,
By Thy grace to be
Just a cleansèd channel
For Thy life through me.

Margaret E. Barber

I think this is one of the best hymns in the world. It was written by Miss Margaret E. Barber of Foochow. The whole composition is highly poetic and the feeling in it very deep. It shows a most matured sentiment.

The first stanza sets the tone. The truth is most accurate, the expressions are very rich, and the spiritual feeling is good.

The second stanza is the best of all. The thought there climbs very high. When the soul says: "If there's less of earth joy," the writer is speaking to herself; that is, she is in communion with herself; but she also is in communion with God, for she continues with: "Give, Lord, more of heaven." In case there is less "earth," give me more of "heaven." "Let the spirit praise Thee, though the heart be riven." You see here how the spirit and the heart differ. The heart may be riven, but the spirit may still praise.

The sentiment continues to climb. "If sweet earthly ties, Lord, break at Thy decree, let the tie that binds us, closer, sweeter, be." The breaking of earthly ties strengthens the tie with the Lord. How delicate is the feeling unveiled here.

Since the writer cannot climb any higher, she returns to conclude with a prayer: "Lonely though the pathway, cheer it with Thy smile; be Thou my companion through earth's little while." Such expressions as, "cheer it with Thy smile" and "through earth's little while" are highly poetic. "Selfless may I live, Lord, by Thy grace to be just a cleansèd channel for Thy life through me." During these days I have only one desire and that is, that I may be selfless, a cleansed channel to live out Your will. How beautiful this hymn is.

The Whole Bible a Poem

In the Bible many poems are not written by words but by deeds. Look at John the Baptist. When he speaks of the Lord, how poetic he is. He says, "He that cometh after me, the latchet of whose shoe I am not worthy to unloose" (John 1:27). This is poetry. If one were rough in feeling, he would say how much lower another person is to himself. Only those who have learned before God can say, "Whose latchet I am not worthy to unloose."

You remember the story of the prodigal son and of how he prepared a long dissertation to deliver upon his return.

"Father, I have sinned against heaven, and in thy sight: I am no more worthy to be called thy son: make me as one of thy hired servants." (Lk. 15:18-19). How unpoetic he is. But look at the father. When he sees the son at a distance, he runs to him. He does not blame his son for wasting all his property; neither does he ask what more he can do for his son. He cuts short his son's speech, and, without saying a word, he kisses his son. Is not that poetic?

Let me tell you: the whole Bible is a poem. Those who are insensitive in their feeling are not able to touch its spirit. We thank God for we know that in the eternity to come our feelings will be much more delicate than those we have today. We know there will be more praises in heaven than prayers on earth. Prayer shall pass away and praise shall fill eternity. How excellent that day will be when all our feelings become exquisite and tender.

Finally, we are not attempting to make brothers and sisters musicians. We are not musicians but we are songsters! Christian hymns help us to develop delicate spiritual feelings. May we so learn that we are able to come to God with a more tender spirit and be brought closer to Him. The Lord be gracious to us.

PRAISE

The Value of Praise

Praise is the greatest work God's children can ever do. It is the loftiest expression the saints can ever show. The highest manifestation of spiritual life is seen in men praising God.

Though the throne of God is the heart of the universe, it is nonetheless established on the praise of the children of God. God's name is exalted through praise. There is nothing a Christian can offer which surpasses praise.

Sacrifice is very important to God, yet "The sacrifice of the wicked is an abomination" (Prov. 21:27). Never, though, do we hear of praise as being abominable. There is abominable sacrifice but never abominable praise.

Prayer also occupies a very big place in the Bible, but we are told that, "He that turneth away his ear from hearing the law, even his prayer is an abomination" (Prov. 28:9). We have never read, however, of any praise being abominable. Is this not quite wonderful? David in his psalms says: "Evening, and morning, and at noon, will I

109

pray and moan aloud; and he will hear my voice" (Ps. 55:17 Darby); also "Seven times a day do I praise thee, because of thy righteous ordinances" (Ps. 119:164). He prays three times a day, but praises seven times a day. As moved by the Holy Spirit, he acknowledges the significance of praise.

PRAISE IS ADDED TO PRIESTLY FUNCTIONS

One thing we know: all matters related to worship, the tabernacle, the sacrifices, and the priesthood are given in detail in the book of Exodus. The pattern shown to Moses in the mount was not open to any addition or subtraction. All who know God know that Moses did not dare add any of his own ideas in building the tabernacle in the wilderness. Since the whole project was divine, no one was allowed to tamper with the pattern. Everything was done exactly according to God's command. Yet years later, David and Solomon seemed to make changes in the priesthood when they added something to the functions of the priests. They appointed a great number of people to the work of praising God. This change, though, was not rejected, but accepted, by God.

This may not surprise you; but if you know the Bible, you know for certain that no man may act carelessly before God. In the Old Testament, those who offered strange fire were burned to death. Even at the time of David, Uzzah was smitten to death for touching the falling ark because Israel used an ox cart to transport it. This was not in accordance with God's instructions. David ought to have known that he did not have the liberty to impose his own ideas into the things of God or into the service of God. Yet we also see him setting up people to praise God in the tabernacle. No fire came from God to burn them up, for this was not considered offering strange fire; neither was anyone smitten as Uzzah had been. This fact indicates that praise is acceptable to God. When praise was introduced into God's service, it was not rejected. Therefore let us remember: there can be abominable prayer and abominable sacrifice, but there is no abominable praise. The throne of the Lord is established on our praises.

PSALMS OF PRAISE

One thing stressed very much and often recorded in the Bible is praise. From the time of the exodus from Egypt, we find incessant praises. The whole collection of the Psalms is full of praises. Moses first composed a song of praise in Exodus 15, and from then on throughout the Old Testament there have been many notes of praise. "Who is like unto thee, O Jehovah, among the gods? Who is like thee, glorious in holiness, fearful in praises, doing wonders?" (Ex. 15:11). God is fearful and worthy to be praised.

Many do not quite comprehend why the collection of the Psalms is in the Bible. It is as if God still is not satisfied with all the praises already found elsewhere. So the Holy Spirit inspired psalmists such as David, Moses, Asaph, and others to offer praises before Him. Their psalms are not just psalms of praise; they are also psalms of suffering. Many record the experience of being brought into the shadow of death, "All thy waves and thy billows are gone over me" (Ps. 42:7). They were forsaken by men and slandered and persecuted by enemies; yet out of these experiences praise ascended to God. These words of praise, therefore, do not come from the mouths of the prosperous, but from those under God's discipline.

All who study the Bible know that of all the books in the Old Testament, the collection of the Psalms expresses most deeply the wounds in the feelings of men. But please remember, even in these very psalms the voices of praise are the loudest and the highest. Out of the many sufferings and persecutions and slanderings, God has composed songs of praises in the lives of His own people. They learn to praise God in all kinds of circumstances.

Do not think that joyful praise is the loudest. Often the loudest praise is from those who have gone through deep distress before God. Such praise is well-accepted and fully blessed by God. This is what He desires every one of us to learn. We must not only raise the note of praise when we stand on the summit and view the promised land of Canaan, but we must also learn to compose psalms of praise when we walk through the valley of the shadow of death. This is truly praise.

Now we can conclude what the true nature of praise is. As we have already said, the book of the Psalms is the only book of praise in the Old Testament. It could be entitled "Praise." Many find their praises in the Psalms. Many Psalms may be sung. During the Old Testament time people did sing the Psalms. But take special note of the fact that they who offered praise in the Old Testament were those whom God had purposely led through distressful situations so that out of their wounded feelings they might compose the words of praise.

The Nature of Praise

Praise in its nature is a sacrifice. If suffering is incidental, then it would not be a part of the nature of praise. But we know suffering is not accidental but planned by God. This means that praise derives its character from suffering and from darkness. Hence the writer of the Hebrews says: "Through him then let us offer up a sacrifice of praise to God continually, that is, the fruit of lips which make confession to his name" (Heb. 13:15).

Brethren, what is a sacrifice? It involves death and loss. He who sacrifices incurs loss. The bullock or the lamb used to be yours, used to be your possession and property. Today you bring it before God as a sacrifice; you suffer its loss. God wants men today to offer praise as if offering a sacrifice. In other words, He enables you to offer praises to Him by wounding you, grinding you, and cutting you deeply. God's throne is established on praises. How will He obtain these praises?—by His children's coming to Him, each bringing the sacrifice of praise.

New believers must learn to praise. We mentioned in an earlier chapter the need to pray to God. Now we shall consider how to praise Him. David received grace to praise God seven times a day. Shall we do so less than that? No, let us praise God incessantly. Let us learn to say, "Lord, I praise You."

When I first believed in the Lord, every evening I would try to recall whether I had praised seven times during the day. If I found myself to have praised only once, I would get up from bed and praise the Lord six more times reverently. Sometimes in the middle of the night, I would awaken and remember I had not praised seven times during that day; I would rise and remedy the defect before I went back to sleep. I believe it is a good practice, an excellent spiritual exercise, for new believers to learn to praise God day after day. Let them learn to praise Him in the early morning, praise Him when they are in trouble, praise Him in the assembly, and praise Him when they are alone. They should praise God at least seven times daily, certainly not less often than David did.

The Sacrifice of Praise

After you have learned to praise the Lord, then there will come a day when you simply cannot do so. You will discover that though you could praise God seven times yesterday and the day before yesterday and a week ago and even a month ago, yet today you cannot praise. It is a dark day, a day without a glimmer of light. You suffer much misunderstanding and endure many slandering words. You feel as if you cannot shed enough tears for yourself. How can you have the strength to praise God? Yet, because you have already learned how to praise God daily, you will also learn the sacrifice of praise. If you had not praised either yesterday or the day before, it would be no surprise if you could not praise today. However, if you have been praising daily during the month, but now, because of your painful environment, you simply cannot praise, then there is a real problem. You may feel that it would be a more natural expression at the moment if you were to fret rather than to praise. You blame the Lord for bringing you into such a situation. Nevertheless, you should remember that the throne of the Lord never changes; His name and His glory change not. Therefore, you must praise Him.

Once you realize that however you may suffer or be in distress, you still must praise God for He is worthy to be praised—at that moment your praise becomes a sacrifice. During that time your praise sounds like the slaughtering of your fattest ox or the binding of your beloved son on the altar. As you insist on saying that the Lord is worthy to be praised, you praise with tears in your eyes. This is the sacrifice of praise.

As soon as one becomes a Christian, he ought to learn to praise God daily. I will give him a rule: he must praise God at least seven times a day. He must see that he cannot praise less than David did. He also needs to be told that he must offer the sacrifice of praise too. Daily he offers his praise. Then one day he enters into darkness. In his distress he discovers how hard it is to open his mouth and praise God. But if during that time he then learns to praise God and to praise Him loudly, he will find that a sacrifice is being offered. Had his feelings not been wounded, he could never have climbed so high toward God. He cannot praise on his own behalf; he praises solely because God is worthy to be praised. Thus his praise turns into a sacrifice. No matter what his circumstances, he continues to praise.

The Way to Victory

First we need to see that praise is a sacrifice. Then we shall see that it is also a way to victory. It is a very common strategy of Satan to attack God's children in the area of prayer. Many brothers and sisters complain to me that they are so frequently under attack they cannot pray very well. We often read in spiritual books that what Satan fears most is God's children in prayer, that he will flee when God's children are on their knees. This is quite familiar to us. But what I would like to say today is, that what Satan attacks most furiously is not prayer, but praise.

I do not say Satan does not attack prayer. When a Christian starts to pray, Satan begins to attack. It is therefore relatively easy to talk with people, but quite difficult to pray. Indeed, Satan does attack prayer. However, he also assaults the praise of God's children. If he could prevent all words of praise from rising up to God, he would gladly use all his strength to do so.

Do remember: whenever God's children are praising, Satan must flee. Prayer frequently is a battle, but praise is victory. Prayer is spiritual warfare; praise is the shout of triumph. For this reason praise is that which Satan hates most. He will exert all his strength to quench our praise whenever possible. The children of God act foolishly when they look at their environment or consider their feelings and then stop praising the Lord. If they really know God, they will see that even in the jail at Philippi there was a place for song. As Paul and Silas were praying and singing hymns unto God, all the doors of the prison opened (Acts 16:25–26). Prayer may not always open prison doors but praise does!

In the book of Acts prison doors were opened twice. The first time it happened was to Peter and the second was to Paul. On the first occasion the church prayed earnestly for Peter, and as a result an angel opened the prison gate and led Peter out. On the second occasion Paul and Silas were singing hymns, praising the Lord; immediately all the

116

doors opened and everyone's bands were loosed. The jailer believed on the Lord that very same night; his whole family was saved and rejoiced greatly in the Lord. Here we find two men offering the sacrifice of praise in prison, even though the wounds on their backs were unhealed, their bodies racked with pain, their feet fastened in the stocks, and their strength not yet restored. Furthermore, the Roman prison was a dark, damp, and gloomy place. Was there anything to be happy about? Any reason to sing? But here were men whose spirits climbed high. They transcended everything and saw that God was still sitting on the throne. We may change, our environment may alter, our feelings may waver, but God never changes. He is still the God who is worthy to be praised. So it was that our brothers Paul and Silas sang hymns. They praised out of their sufferings. Such praise cost them much; therefore it was both a sacrifice of praise and a note of triumph.

Why is praise also triumph? Because when you pray, you are yet in the environment; but when you praise, you have risen above the environment. Whenever you are praying and pleading, you are involved in the thing you ask for. The more you plead, the more you are bound by that thing, for it is before you all the time. But if you are brought by God beyond the prison, beyond the stocks, beyond the shame and suffering, then you are able to raise your voice and sing praise to the name of God.

What prayer may fail to accomplish, praise can. This is a basic principle to be remembered. If you cannot pray, why not praise? The Lord has not only given us prayer but also praise that through it we may claim the victory. "But thanks be unto God, who always leadeth us in triumph in Christ" (2 Cor. 2:14). Whenever your spirit is pressed beyond measure so that you can hardly breathe, let alone pray, why do you not try to praise God? Pray when you are able to pray; but praise when you cannot pray.

We usually think that as long as a burden is heavy we should pray, and then when the prayer is over it is time to praise. Indeed when a burden is heavy we should pray, yet sometimes it becomes so heavy that we are unable to do so. This then, is the time to praise. Do not wait until the burden is over before you start to praise. Rather, let us praise when the burden becomes too heavy. Frequently in facing difficult situations, our whole being seems paralyzed. We are perplexed as to what we should do. May I suggest that this is the time to learn to praise? Here is the very best opportunity. If you praise at this moment, the Spirit of God will begin to work to bring you to the place where all the doors open and every chain falls off. He who sings is free; though he be put to shame, being literally bound, he is still free and able to sing. Thus he transcends every situation; nothing—no person or thing—can cause him to be downhearted.

New believers should learn this kind of praise at the very beginning of their Christian life. It is not the ordinary kind of praise, but a sacrifice with pain and suffering in it. In offering the sacrifice of praise, one puts himself into a triumphant position. Let young believers always maintain an ascendant spirit, thus transcending the attacking evil spirit. Then it will be that nothing, neither the world nor the environment, will be able to separate them from God. Prayer may fail to touch the throne, but praise always enables us to do so. Prayer does not guarantee victory at all times, but praise is never defeated.

God's children ought to open their mouths and praise

Him. Let it be not only in times of calm and peace but especially in times of turmoil and suffering. You should lift up your head in the most difficult situation and say, "Lord, I praise You." Tears may fall from your eyes, but praise flows from your heart. Though your heart is wounded, your mouth yet pours forth praise. In praising, you ascend and join yourself to the One whom you praise. It is foolish to murmur. The more you murmur, the deeper you are buried in your trouble. The more you fret, the greater the pressure you build up within until the environment and problems almost overcome you.

Some people (perhaps you are among them) are more advanced spiritually. In times of trouble, you pray instead of murmuring. Prayer to you means struggling, for you strive strenuously to get above the situation. You refuse to be buried by your environment or by your feelings, so you pray in order to rise above these things. Such prayer does sometimes prevail. But if it fails to extricate you, then praise alone can set you free. When you offer the sacrifice of praise, that is, offer praise as a sacrifice, you will quickly transcend everything; nothing can bury you.

Praise and Warfare

Let us look at another important passage concerning praise. It is found in 2 Chronicles 20:20-22.

And they rose early in the morning, and went forth into the wilderness of Tekoa: and as they went forth, Jehoshaphat stood and said, Hear me, O Judah, and ye inhabitants of Jerusalem: believe in Jehovah your God, so shall ye be established; believe his prophets, so shall ye prosper. And when he had taken counsel with the people, he appointed

119

them that should sing unto Jehovah, and give praise in holy array, as they went out before the army, and say, Give thanks unto Jehovah; for his lovingkindness endureth for ever. And when they began to sing and to praise, Jehovah set liers-in-wait against the children of Ammon, Moab, and mount Seir, that were come against Judah; and they were smitten.

Here we find a war going on. Jehoshaphat reigned during the closing years of the nation of Judah. The country was exceedingly weak and wholly unable to defend herself against the attack of Ammon, Moab, and the children of Mount Seir. She would be badly beaten, even completely destroyed. Yet Jehoshaphat feared God and because of this, there was a revival during his reign. Though he was not perfect, he nonetheless desired after God. He exhorted his people to trust Him. How were they to meet their enemies? Not by sending an army to fight the foe, but by setting up singers to praise the Lord. Those who would do the singing in praise of the Lord should be clothed in holy array. They would walk before the army and say, "Give thanks unto Jehovah; for his lovingkindness endureth for ever."

Please notice the word "began"; at the very moment when God's people sang and praised, the Lord smote the Ammonites, the Moabites, and the people of Mount Seir.

Here we learn a great lesson. Victory is not due to fighting but to praising. We ought to discover how to defeat the enemy by praising the Lord. It is not only through prayer but also through praise. When our faith is feeble, we feel we must pray much; but when our faith is strengthened, we are able to praise more. Many, realizing the fierceness of the enemy and their own weakness, attempt to struggle and to pray. They fail to recognize this wonderful principle that victory is not dependent on fighting.

The children of God are often subject to the temptation to fight. They assume that they will not be able to overcome unless they fight. They are beset with almost insurmountable difficulties, for they have to deal with each case and each person. They must find one way to deal with the Ammonites, another for the Moabites, and still another for the people of Mount Seir. They are involved with methods and people. Let us remember, though, that the more we get involved with method, the less we are able to overcome. Why? Because this puts us on the same footing and in the same battlefield as those with whom we have to deal. We stand on one side and they on the other. We all are on similar ground. An army here and an army there, and thus we fight. In such circumstances, it is not very easy to overcome. But an altogether different situation arises when we have an army here and a chorus there. There is no fighting, for singers are not warriors. If these singers had not been firm believers in God, they would have to have been insane. But they were not insane, for they were believers. Praise God, we too are not insane but true believers in God.

Young believers should start to learn this lesson right away. You do not need to wait for many years before you begin to learn the lesson of praise. It is something to be acquired at the very beginning of the Christian life. Every time you meet a problem, ask for God's mercy to keep your hands from making war preparations and to keep your mind from conceiving methods of doing battle. Let Him keep you so that you have no scheme hidden within nor any overt action without. Many battles are won by praise, as many defeats are caused by the absence of it.

If you trust in God, in the hour of distress you will be able to say, "I praise Your name. Though my problems are greater than my ability, You are greater than my problems. They are strong, but You are stronger. Your lovingkindness endures forever." There is a holy elevation in praising God. Praise rises higher than prayer. Those who praise do not rest on expectation; they already have transcended. They have praised until the victory has been won.

"When they began to sing and to praise, Jehovah set liers-in-wait . . . and they were smitten." I believe that nothing moves the Lord's hand so much or so fast as praise does. There are many times when we need to pray. I do not in the least want to suggest that we can dispense with prayer. No, we need to pray. We definitely encourage young believers to pray thoroughly and daily. Nevertheless, there are many matters which are overcome only through praise.

I humbly acknowledge that many of God's children whom I know share this experience with me. Many are severely tested under continuous trials. When the testing gets rugged and the battle becomes fierce, then one is in the same predicament as Jehoshaphat. During such a time everything seems to be lost. The one side is so strong while the other side is so weak that there can hardly be any comparison. One feels as if he were wrapped up in a whirlwind. The problem is too big for him to overcome. At that moment it is natural for him to focus his thoughts on his difficulty. His eyes see nothing but his problem.

The more one is tested, the more he takes account of what is left. To many widows, the handful of meal in the jar and the little bit of oil in the cruse are far more important than all that may be kept in the storehouse (see 1 Kings 17). As one's trial increases, so does his apprehension of the difficulty. He always notices how little there is left for him. This moment, when one looks at himself and at his environment, is the moment of the greatest trial. The more one is tried, the more he looks at himself and his environment. But it is not so with those who know God. Trials only turn their eyes to the Lord. The more trials they have, the more they praise.

We must learn not to look at ourselves. Our eyes should look to the Lord. Let us lift up our heads and say, "Lord, You far transcend all. We will praise You." Allow me to say, such loud praise, praise which comes from the heart, praise which flows out of suffering, is the sacrifice of praise, well-pleasing and acceptable to God. God never turns away from the sacrifice of praise. Such a sacrifice ascends to God instantly and the enemy is defeated by it.

The Basic Substance of Praise

In Psalm 106 which depicts the situation of the Israelites in the wilderness, there is one word which is most precious: "Then believed they his words; they sang his praise" (v. 12). They believed, therefore they sang; they believed, so they praised. Within praise there is the basic content of faith. No one should lightly praise or casually say, "I thank the Lord; I praise the Lord!" No, such words cannot be reckoned as praise, for praise must be substantiated by faith. In a time of distress you pray; when in sorrow you pray. You pray and pray until you are able to believe in your heart. Then you open your mouth to praise.

Praise, therefore, is living. It is not something carelessly uttered. Whenever one is troubled, he ought to pray. But once there rises within you a little faith enabling you to believe in God, in His power, greatness, mercy, and glory, then you should start to praise. Remember, if one has faith within him and fails to praise, that faith will sooner or later fade away. I make this statement on the basis of experience. Let me say it most emphatically: if you find faith in you, you must praise, or else you will soon lose the faith.

Young believers need to know that they should start praising after they have prayed enough to find faith rising in their hearts and are assured of their prayers being answered. They should praise, saying "Lord, I thank You and I praise You, for this matter is already settled." Do not wait till the thing has come to pass before you praise. Praise as soon as faith is found. Do not sing after the enemy has fled, but sing to make him flee. We do not invite the singers to come and have a thanksgiving convocation after the Moabites and the Ammonites have retreated; rather, open the thanksgiving meeting in order to drive the Moabites away. We praise Him not after our foes have fled but before then. Then, as we are praising Him, we shall see our enemies completely routed. Verse twelve in Psalm 106 shows us the need for faith. Faith precedes praise, and praise brings in victory.

Human thoughts are generally occupied with struggling and fighting because man always has the enemy in sight. But divine thought is centered on faith and praise; it thinks only of God. Man cannot forget to strive and to fight because his eyes are occupied with the enemy. But if the glory of God were to fill his eyes, he would then believe in God. His spirit, being filled with the glory of God, would turn to praise. The enormity of the enemy thus diminishes; his importance is reduced to nothingness. Let us see that God transcends all. Therefore He deserves our praise.

The Practice of Praise

It is expected that you will learn how to praise. In times of distress, learn to utter words of praise. Even the thought of praising is not enough; it needs to be expressed in words. You should praise when you have no feeling until you do have feeling, and then from little feeling to much feeling. Praise from a little bit of faith to the faith that transcends all. Declare before the enemy, before distress and problems, saying "Oh, Lord, I praise You!" Praise until you are fully inspired.

Nothing possesses so much power to push away the enemy as praise does. Only praise can rout the foe. The sacrifice of praise is most effectual before God. You know what a sacrifice means—it is bringing a sheep or a bullock to be slaughtered before the Lord. In the early days the Israelites would even pawn or sell their goods in order to obtain sheep or bullocks for an offering to God. This is the meaning of sacrifice. In like manner, I today offer words which represent the best of my feeling, words which come from my innermost being, saying "God, I praise You and I thank You." Let me tell you, in such a situation, no enemy will be able to stand; he is forced to flee. Victory thus obtained is real; praise alone gives true victory.

Let us analyze a little. Our problems are of two kinds. The first kind is environmental or accidental, such as the problem which Jehoshaphat faced. This type of problem is overcome by faith. The other kind is problems of a personal nature, such as the suffering of being hurt, offended, and humiliated by others. This is a matter of personal overcoming in regard to unreasonable treatment, irrational affront, causeless hatred, or baseless slander. How very difficult it is for brothers and sisters to overcome these undeserved disgraces. One's whole being struggles against such mistreatment; one's soul revolts against it. How difficult it is to forgive and how hard to overcome.

How can we overcome these personal problems? Prayer does not seem to avail much when you are pressed with misunderstanding, slander, and persecution. I myself have prayed and I know. Many have prayed and found it of little effect. It is futile to resist and to strive. The more you refuse to be pressed, the more you are oppressed. You suffer intensely and you find it hard to overcome. Therefore I want to suggest that you turn to praise.

Remember, when personal problems are greatest, when misunderstandings are at their height, and when abuses are the most unreasonable—remember, this is the time to give thanks, not to pray. You should bow your head and say to the Lord, "Lord, I thank You. I receive this mistreatment from Your hand, and I praise You for it all." By so doing, you will find everything is transcended. Victory does not lie in struggling with your flesh, trying to see if you can ever forgive. It comes when you lower your head and praise the Lord, saying, "Lord, I praise Your way. What You have arranged for me cannot be wrong. Whatever You do is perfect." As you thus praise the Lord, your spirit transcends, rising above your problems and above your own inner feelings.

Those who feel hurt are those who do not praise. If you are able to come to the Lord and praise Him, all your hurt feelings will be transformed into sentiments of praise. You have climbed high if you can say before God, "I thank You and I praise You. There is no mistake in what You have done." Walking in this way, you leave everything behind you. How glorious this path is, the path of the sacrifice of praise. Gone are all problems with the Lord, with any brother or sister, and even with your own self. Therefore, praise. The Christian life ascends through praise. Learn to present the sacrifice of praise and also help the brethren to do the same.

Nothing helps people to mature as does the sacrifice of praise. Forgive me for saying this, but I believe there is absolutely nothing which matures and sweetens and mellows people as much as the sacrifice of praise. One may see in these people's lives not only the discipline of the Holy Spirit but even praise for that discipline. You see not just the hand of the Lord upon you, but you also sing because of His hand. You are not simply chastised, but you accept the chastisement thankfully. Because you have learned to praise, the door to glory has opened before you.

The Bible speaks so much on this matter of praise that it is impossible for us to deal with it in detail. We only desire that you may, before God, truly see how praise is basically a sacrifice. As children of God, we ought to praise.

Glorifies God

Finally, I wish to read with you one passage found in Psalm 50: "Whoso offereth the sacrifice of thanksgiving glorifieth me" (v. 23). The Lord is seeking our praises. Nothing glorifies God more than praise. We know that one day all prayer shall become a thing of the past, all works shall have passed away. Prophecy shall be gone, labors shall cease. But in that day, praise shall be increased far above that of today. It shall continue without end. Praise will never cease. In heaven, in our heavenly home, we shall praise more and learn more how to praise God. I believe it is best that we start to learn this most excellent lesson right here on earth.

Concerning the matter of glorifying God, I have a thought to share. Today we see in a mirror darkly; though we see a little, yet we cannot understand the full meaning for it has been distorted. We feel great pain for the things we have suffered, not recognizing the difference between inward hurt and circumstantial difficulty. Since we do not understand, we find it hard to praise. I believe the abundance of praise in heaven is due to our perfect knowledge there. The more perfect the knowledge, the greater the praise. One day when we all come to the presence of the Lord, everything will be crystal clear. What is a puzzle to us now will be solved then. On that day we shall be able to see His hand in every step of the discipline of the Holy Spirit. Had the Holy Spirit's discipline been lacking, to what depths would we have fallen! If He had not restrained our steps, where would we have been?

If we realize this, we will bow our heads in praise saying "Lord, You are never wrong." Every step in the discipline of the Holy Spirit is an indication of God's painstaking effort with us. Had I not been sick such-and-such a time, I do not know what would have become of me. Had I not fallen that time, I do not know where I would be. Though what I have experienced has been distressful, yet what I have avoided would have meant even greater distress. Today we murmur, but on that day we shall see why God apportioned to us what He did. Each step we take today is under His guidance. In the day to come we shall prostrate ourselves, saying, "What a fool I was that I did not praise You." How ashamed we will be in that day if today, instead of praise and thanks, we murmur.

So let us learn even today to say, "You can never be wrong. Although I do not understand, I know that whatever You do is right." Learn to believe; then you will be able to praise. How grateful we will be on the day when we can confess: "Lord, I thank You for Your grace in delivering me from unnecessary fret and murmur. Lord, I do thank You for the grace which keeps me from uttering murmuring words."

Let us see now the goodness of God. We praise Him because He is good. Let us first learn to believe that the Lord is good, that He never can be wrong. Believing, we are able to praise. And "Whoso offereth the sacrifice of thanksgiving glorifieth me." May all new believers learn this lesson at the commencement of their Christian journey. I learned this lesson during the first two years of my Christian life. After more than twenty years, I have much cause to thank Him. I have peace within me, for I know the importance of praise. Many times in defeat, in murmur, and in discontent, light comes from the Lord and instantly I see that He sits on the throne and that therefore it is time to praise. Many are the difficulties overcome through praise. Help young believers to be people of praise at the very outset. Learn to praise from the heart. "Whoso offereth the sacrifice of thanksgiving glorifieth me." God is worthy to be glorified.

THE BREAKING OF BREAD

The cup of blessing which we bless, is it not a communion of the blood of Christ? The bread which we break, is it not a communion of the body of Christ? seeing that we, who are many, are one bread, one body: for we all partake of the one bread. Behold Israel after the flesh: have not they that eat the sacrifices communion with the altar? What say I then? that a thing sacrificed to idols is anything, or that an idol is anything? But I say, that the things which the Gentiles sacrifice, they sacrifice to demons, and not to God: and I would not that ye should have communions with demons. Ye cannot drink the cup of the Lord, and the cup of demons: ye cannot partake of the table of the Lord, and of the table of demons. Or do we provoke the Lord to jealousy? are we stronger than he?

1 Cor. 10:16-22

For I received of the Lord that which also I delivered unto you, that the Lord Jesus in the night in which he was betrayed took bread; and when he had given thanks, he brake it, and said, This is my body, which is for you: this do in remembrance of me. In like manner also the cup, after supper, saying, This cup is the new covenant in my blood: this do, as often as ye drink it, in remembrance of me. For as often as ye eat this bread, and drink the cup, ye proclaim the Lord's death till he come. Wherefore whosoever shall eat the bread or drink the cup of the Lord in an unworthy manner, shall be guilty of the body and the blood of the Lord. But let a man prove himself, and so let him eat of the bread, and drink of the cup. For he that eateth and drinketh, eateth and drinketh judgment unto himself, if he discern not the body. For this cause many among you are weak and sickly, and not a few sleep. But if we discerned ourselves, we should not be judged. But when we are judged, we are chastened of the Lord, that we may not be condemned with the world. Wherefore, my brethren, when ye come together to eat, wait one for another.

1 Cor. 11:23-33

In this chapter we will consider the matter of the Lord's table or the Lord's supper.

The Supper Instituted by the Lord

Let us first see how the Lord instituted the supper. This is one supper which all the children of God in the church must attend. It was set up by the Lord Jesus on the night before His death. Since He was crucified the next day, this was His last night on earth and also His last supper with His disciples. Although He still ate after His resurrection, this nevertheless was His last supper, for a resurrected man can either eat or not, as he chooses.

How did this last supper come about? The Jews keep a festival called the Passover which commemorates their deliverance by God from slavery in Egypt. God commanded them to prepare a lamb for each house and in the evening of the fourteenth day of the first month they were to kill the lamb and put its blood on the two side-posts and on the lintel. They should eat the flesh on that night with unleavened bread and bitter herbs. After they came out of

Egypt, they were ordered to keep the feast each year as a remembrance. So, to the Jews the paschal lamb is something retrospective. Because of God's great deliverance, they recall that great event every year.

It so happened that the night before the death of the Lord Jesus coincided with the eating of the paschal lamb. There was nothing special in His taking the paschal lamb with the disciples, for it was simply keeping the feast of the Passover. But immediately afterwards, the Lord established His own supper, thus implying that He desires us to partake of His supper even as the Jews eat the paschal lamb.

As we compare these two, we see that the Israelites keep the Passover because they were delivered out of Egypt, and that God's children today partake of the Lord's table because they too have been delivered. The Israelites had a lamb; we too have the Lamb whom God appointed. We have today been saved from the world, delivered from the power of Satan, and become wholly God's. We keep this feast as the Jews kept the Passover.

1. Supper Is a Family Meal

What does supper signify? Why do we call it the Lord's supper? It is a worldwide custom that supper is especially considered a family meal. At lunch, the members of the family often cannot assemble together. In the land of Judea at noontime, some of the family would be shepherding, some fishing, and some tilling. Most of them would eat their lunch outside, for it would be impossible to go home. So lunch is not a family meal. Neither is breakfast a family meal for at that time people are thinking of the day's work instead of the rest afterward. Other than those who are sick, people usually take their breakfast hastily. Supper, however, is the most special of the three daily meals, for at that meal the whole family, young and old, gathers together to eat.

2. SUPPER EXCLUDES THE THOUGHT OF WORK

Having finished a day's work, people no longer think of the work before them; rather, they are occupied with the thought of rest. Supper is the time when the whole family gathers together and eats at leisure after the day's work is done. In instituting His own supper, our Lord desired His people throughout the earth to see that this is, indeed, a family meal in God's house. It does not include any idea of work. It just sets forth the thought of rest. During breakfast and lunch, one's mind is always occupied with work; but by supper, everything has been done. One is prepared to retire after eating. God's children should gather and partake of the Lord's supper with a similar inward sentiment.

Dual Meaning of the Lord's Supper

1. REMEMBER THE LORD

The basic thought of the Lord's supper is to remember the Lord. The Lord Himself says, "This do in remembrance of me" (1 Cor. 11:24b). He knows how very forgetful we are. Do not think that because we have received such an abundance of grace and experienced such a wonderful redemption that we will never be able to forget. Let me warn you that men such as we, are most forgetful. For this reason, the Lord especially desires us both to remember Him and to remember what He has done for us.

The Lord wants us to remember Him not only because we are so forgetful, but also because He needs our memory. In other words, He does not want us to forget Him. The Lord is so great and so transcendant that He could let us forget Him and not be bothered by it. Yet He says, "This do in remembrance of me," thus revealing how condescending He is in desiring our remembrance.

That the Lord wants us to remember Him fully is an expression of His love. It is the demand of love, not of greatness. So far as His greatness is concerned, He can afford to be forgotten by us. But His love insists that we remember Him. If we do not remember Him, we will suffer great loss. If we do not remember Him often and keep the redemption of the Lord always before us, we will easily be conformed to the world and become contentious toward the children of God. Thus we not only need to remember Him, but are profited by so doing. It is a means by which we may receive the grace of the Lord.

In connection with the Lord's desire for us to remember Him, there is another point worth noticing: as the Lord formerly humbled Himself in order to be our Savior, so today He humbles Himself in asking for our remembrance. As once He condescended to save us, so today He condescends to ask for our hearts. He wishes us to remember Him as long as we live on earth. He wants us to live before Him and remember Him week after week. Thus we derive much spiritual benefit.

DISASSOCIATES YOU FROM THE WORLD

One cardinal value in remembering the Lord lies in the fact that the world will not be able to exert its influence continuously upon you. If every few days you remember how the Lord died for you and received you, let me tell you, the world will have no place in you. Since my Lord suffered death here in the world, what have I to say? If they had not killed my Lord, there might still be some ground for them to talk with me. But now that they have already killed my Lord and His death is exhibited before me, I have nothing more to say and no way to communicate with the world. I cannot have any fellowship with it. This is one of the prime benefits of the breaking of bread.

DISPELS DIVISION

Remembering the Lord has another spiritual value: it makes strife and contention and division impossible among God's children. When you are reminded of how you have been saved by grace and you find another person with you who is likewise reminded, you are both one before the Lord. When you contemplate how the Lord Jesus forgave the myriads of your sins and you see another brother coming to the supper who has also been bought and redeemed by the precious blood, how can you bring in anything to separate you from him? How can you divide God's children? For the past nearly two thousand years, many controversies among God's children have been settled at the Lord's supper. Many unforgiven things, even things unforgivable, and many lifelong hatreds have disappeared at the Lord's table, for it is impossible not to forgive when, in remembering the Lord, you are reminded of how you have been saved and forgiven. Can you be forgiven your debt of ten thousand talents ($10,000,000) by the Lord and yet grab another servant by the throat demanding payment for a hundred shillings ($18) (see Matt. 18:4–35)?

ENLARGES YOUR HEART

Another advantage in remembering the Lord is that each one who remembers Him will quite naturally have his heart enlarged to embrace all children of God. It is but natural to see that all who are redeemed by the Lord's blood are the beloved of the Lord; therefore they are also the delight of my heart. If we are all in the Lord, can there be jealousy, reviling and unforgivingness? How can you continue in strife with the brother or sister who sits next to you at the Lord's supper? What right do you have to demand anything of your brother when you recall how many of your sins have been forgiven? If you insist on strife, jealousy, and an unforgiving spirit, you will not be able to remember the Lord.

Every time we gather to remember the Lord, we are bidden to review His love once more. We should re-examine the corruption of the world and the judgment upon it. We should renew the conviction that all the redeemed are beloved of the Lord. Every time we remember the Lord, we review His love, how He loved us and gave Himself for us. In love, He descended to hades for us. The world has already been judged, for it crucified our Lord. But all of God's children are our delight, because they have all been bought by the Lord's blood. How can we hate them? How can we harbor any thought of hate?

All that we have mentioned above is included in the meaning of remembering the Lord. The first and foremost significance of the Lord's supper is, "This do in remembrance of me." Let us further point out that it is absolutely impossible for us to remember one whom we do not know or of whom we have no experience. For us to remember a person or an event presumes that we have a personal knowledge of him or of it. So, when the Lord commands us to remember Him, He is merely reminding those of us who have already met Him at Calvary and have received grace from Him. We come to remember all that He has done for us. Like the Jews remembering the Passover, we consider in retrospect. Because we have come out of Egypt, therefore we come together to remember this fact. To remember is to look back.

2. PROCLAIM THE LORD'S DEATH

The Lord's supper has a second meaning. This is found in 1 Corinthians 11:26: "For as often as ye eat this bread, and drink the cup, ye proclaim the Lord's death till he come." We need to proclaim or exhibit the Lord's death that all may see.

What causes people to be idle or unfruitful? It is that they have forgotten the cleansing of their former sins (see 2 Pet. 1:8-9). For this reason the Lord calls us to remember Him, saying, "So long as you live on earth, you must love Me and constantly remember Me. Remember that the cup is My shed blood and the bread My broken body." This refers to our experience, and this must come first. Afterward we have the teaching that the cup and the bread exhibit the death of the Lord.

Why do the cup and the bread represent the Lord's death? Because the blood is in the flesh. So when blood and flesh are separated, it means death. Today the blood and the flesh are separated, for the blood is in the cup while the flesh is in the bread. When one looks at the wine in the cup, he sees the blood. Likewise, when he looks at the bread, he sees the flesh. Thus he does not need to be told that His Lord has died for him. As he notices that the blood is no longer in the flesh, he realizes that death has come. Must the Lord tell you that He has died for you? No, He only needs to say, "Drink the cup and eat the bread," for these proclaim His death. Blood here and flesh there—this speaks of death.

What do the eating of the bread and the drinking of the cup signify? The Old Testament informs us clearly that the bread was made of grain. The same word was used when the Lord told the Israelites that after they entered into Canaan they would eat the old grain of the land. In looking at the bread, you see that the grain has been crushed. In looking at the cup, you see that the grape has been pressed. In this crushed grain and this pressed grape, you see death. Hence the Lord says, eat the bread and drink the cup.

Except a grain of wheat fall into the ground and die, it is but one grain. Likewise, unless a grain of wheat is crushed, it remains a grain and cannot be made into bread. Unless a cluster of grapes is pressed, there will be no wine. The Lord, speaking through Paul, says that as you eat the bread and drink the cup, you are proclaiming His death. If the grain wanted to preserve itself whole, there would not be any bread; if the grape insisted on keeping itself intact, there would not be any wine. It is only as you eat the crushed grain and the pressed grape that you proclaim the Lord's death.

From a human standpoint, God has left nothing on the earth other than the cross. The work of the cross is finished but the sign of the cross remains. Indeed, many today have forgotten the cross, but not the believers. To them, the cross is something forever remembered. Every Lord's day we see in the Lord's supper the cross of the Son of God e. hibited in the church. This suggests that though we may forget everything else, we must remember the fact of our Lord's death for us.

Suppose you bring your parents, children, or relatives who do not know the Lord to the gathering for the breaking of bread. Seeing such a meeting for the first time, they invariably will ask, "What is the meaning of the breaking of bread and the drinking of the cup?" You answer, "The cup represents the blood and the bread the flesh. Since the blood and the flesh are separated, this is death." To those unbelievers who come to the meeting, you point out that in so doing you exhibit the Lord's death.

We not only must go out to preach the gospel, gather people in to hear the glad tidings, and have the word preached by those who are gifted, but we also must let the Lord's table proclaim the good news. It is a great thing if we can convince people that what is placed before them is not a ritual but an exhibition of the Lord's death.

We must proclaim this death until the Lord comes again. I like this thought for it associates the supper with the Lord's return. I wonder if you appreciate the supper. Supper is the last meal of the day. Daily I take my supper; the Lord's supper I take weekly. The night is dark and the day has yet to dawn. For these two thousand years, the church has never eaten breakfast. She has been and still is only taking supper, the last meal. Till He comes, the night remains dark. But soon the day shall dawn, and no one will need to eat supper again. Who eats supper in the early morning? Soon we shall see the Lord face to face. Remembrance will be lost in sight. We will see Him whom we love.

May we see from the beginning that in remembering the Lord we are remembering the Lord's death. This will naturally turn our eyes toward the kingdom, toward the day when we will go to be with the Lord. The cross always leads us to His return; it invariably ends in glory. No one can remember the Lord's death without lifting up his head, without saying, "Lord, I want to see Your face." When the day comes that we do see His face, all things (including this remembrance) shall pass away. So, in remembering the Lord, we exhibit His death till He come. Today we have nothing to do but to wait for His return.

Meaning of the Lord's Table

1 Corinthians 11 speaks of the Lord's supper with its dual meaning of remembering the Lord and exhibiting the Lord's death. Chapter 10 of the same book, however, speaks of it as the Lord's table. Though the subject is the same, yet two different designations are used. Like the Lord's supper, the Lord's table also has a double meaning "The cup of blessing which we bless, is it not a communion of the blood of Christ? The bread which we break, is it not a communion of the body of Christ? seeing that we, who are many, are one bread, one body: for we all partake of the one bread" (vv. 16-17). Here the table carries a double significance: first communion, then oneness.

1. COMMUNION

The first and primary meaning of the Lord's table is communion. "The cup of blessing which we bless, is it not a communion of the blood of Christ?" As 1 Corinthians 11 delves into the relationship of the believer with the Lord, so 1 Corinthians 10 deals with relationships among believers. The former (chapter 11) does not touch upon our mutual relationships; it merely stresses remembering the Lord and proclaiming the Lord's death till He come. The latter (chapter 10), nevertheless emphasizes the communion of the blood of Christ.

Notice that the cup of blessing which we bless is singular in number. We all drink out of the same cup; therefore it demonstrates the sense of communion. Unless people are very intimate, they will not drink from the same cup. That so many of God's children drink from the same cup, fully attests to the communion aspect of the Lord's table.

In chapter 11 our eyes are focused on the Lord, but in chapter 10 we see our brethren. We see them in the cup. The cup is for drinking, and we all drink of the same cup. In so doing we have communion with all of God's children. Let us be careful to not lose sight of this aspect.

2. ONENESS

The second meaning of the Lord's table is oneness. "Seeing that we, who are many, are one bread, one body: for we all partake of the one bread" (v. 17). In this we can see at once that all the children of God are one. The bread of chapter 11 and that of chapter 10 have different emphases. Whereas in chapter 11 the Lord says, "This is my body which is for you. . . ." (v. 24), thus making reference to the bread as His physical body, in chapter 10 the verse reads, "We, who are many, are one bread, one body," this time suggesting that the church is the bread.

Even as we need to learn before the Lord the various meanings of the Lord's table as remembrance, exhibition, and communion, so also we must learn its meaning as oneness. All God's children are as one as the bread is one. We have only one loaf; each believer breaks off a piece. If it were possible to gather all the broken pieces, we could restore that one loaf of bread. The bread scattered among many would still be one loaf if the pieces were reunited. Physically, after the bread is broken and eaten, it cannot be recovered. But spiritually, we are yet one in the Holy Spirit. The Holy Spirit gives Christ to us; yet Christ is still in the Holy Spirit. What has been distributed is the bread, but in the Holy Spirit we are still one and have never been divided. So in the breaking of bread, we confess that the children of God are one. This bread signifies the oneness of the church of God.

The basic problem with the Lord's table lies in the bread. As God's children gather together to break bread, if the bread only represents themselves, it is too small; it should not be broken. The bread must stand for the whole church, including all the children of God on earth as well as those in your particular locality. Hence, it testifies to the oneness of all the children of God.

Some Practical Problems

We have shown brothers and sisters that the meaning of the breaking of bread is twofold: vertically, it is remembering the Lord and proclaiming His death till He come; horizontally, it is communion with all God's children and oneness with them. Since all God's children are redeemed by the precious blood and are included in the bread, we ought to have our hearts enlarged each time we break the bread. Many though we are, yet we are one bread. At no time should we harbor the desire to exclude any brother or any certain group of Christians from the bread. Let me tell you, with the bread it is impossible for you to be a small person.

THE PRINCIPLE OF RECEIVING

How, then, do we receive people to the table of the Lord? Remember, we are not the hosts; we are at best but ushers. This is the Lord's supper, the Lord's table, not ours. We have no authority whatsoever over the Lord's table. We are privileged to eat the bread and drink the cup, but we cannot withhold it from others. We cannot forbid any of the blood-redeemed ones from coming to the Lord's table. We have no authority to refuse it to anyone. We cannot refuse those whom the Lord has received, nor can we reject those who belong to the Lord. We can only refuse those whom the Lord refuses or those who do not belong to Him. The Lord only refuses those who do not belong to Him or those who yet remain in sin. Since their communion with the Lord is already interrupted, we, too, do not have fellowship with them. But let us take note that we are the Lord's and have no authority to exercise other than that which the Lord exercises.

Every time we break the bread, we should think of all those who have received grace. We should not think only of those brothers and sisters whom we personally know. If those gathered at the table in one place refuse to have fellowship with God's children in other places, they are too exclusive.

We hope the hearts of brothers and sisters in every place will be so enlarged that they can embrace all the children of God. To stand on the ground of the church is not to discriminate against any of God's children, as if some were welcome and others not. Every time we come to the Lord's table, we are enabled to see Him once more; thus our hearts are enlarged once again to include all the children of God. The heart is a great mystery. It does not expand by itself; rather it tends to become narrowed by the least bit of carelessness. Its natural inclination is to contract, not to expand. But at the time of remembering the Lord, our hearts should be expanded.

Things to Watch

Finally, we would like to mention a few more things which we should notice at the breaking of bread.

1. ONLY BLESSING AND THANKSGIVING, NO ASKING

In this meeting a special situation exists. We come as those who have been washed by the blood of the Lord— not as those asking for His cleansing. We come as those who have the Lord as our life—not as those asking Him to give us life. Therefore, in such a meeting there is only thanksgiving, no asking. "The cup of blessing which we bless"—we bless what the Lord has already blessed. So the proper note in this meeting is to give thanks, to thank and praise the Lord. It is not the time to ask or plead for anything. Nor is it a time to gather to hear a message. We come for one thing—to remember the Lord; therefore neither prayer nor preaching is proper. It may be allowable to speak briefly on things which have a direct bearing on the Lord Himself, but all other kinds of preaching will only interfere. That which is normal for the meeting is praise and thanks. This is true in chapter 10 of 1 Corinthians as well as in chapter 11.

2. ON THE FIRST DAY OF THE WEEK

When the Lord instituted the supper, He exhorted us to do it often. After resurrection, He broke bread with the two disciples in Emmaus on the first day of the week (Lk. 24:1, 30). The early church also broke bread on the first day of the week (Acts 20:7). There is sufficient example in the church and in the Word of God to show that the breaking of bread should be done on the first day of the week. The Passover comes only once a year, but the breaking of bread comes once every week. Our Lord is not dead but alive; therefore we remember Him on the resurrection day. The first day of the week is indeed a very special day for the church.

3. IN A WORTHY MANNER

"Wherefore whosoever shall eat the bread or drink the cup of the Lord in an unworthy manner, shall be guilty of the body and blood of the Lord. But let a man prove himself, and so let him eat of the bread, and drink of the cup. For he that eateth and drinketh, eateth and drinketh judgment unto himself if he discern not the body" (1 Cor. 11:27-29). It is extremely important that we eat and drink worthily. This does not refer to the person's own worthiness but to the way in which he partakes. A person's worthiness is already taken care of in his being redeemed by the precious blood. If he is not the Lord's, he cannot have any part in the Lord's table. But some who are the Lord's may eat in an unworthy manner; that is, they may receive the bread casually without discerning the Lord's body.

Therefore we exhort young believers to receive the

bread respectfully. You are qualified before God to come, but you are asked by the Lord to examine yourself. You must discern that this is the Lord's body. Hence you cannot take it lightly. You must receive it in a manner worthy of the Lord's body. Since the Lord gives His blood and His flesh to you, you need to receive them respectfully. No one but a fool would despise what God has given to him.